Computer Graphics for the IBM PC

Computer Graphics for the IBM PC

L. Ammeraal

Christelijke Hogere Technische School
Hilversum, The Netherlands

JOHN WILEY & SONS

Chichester • New York • Brisbane • Toronto • Singapore

Library of Congress Cataloging-in-Publication Data:
Ammeraal, L. (Leendert)
  Computer graphics for the IBM PC.
  Bibliography: p.
  Includes index.
  1. IBM Personal Computer—Programming.
2. Computer graphics.   I. Title.
QA76.8.I2594A48   1987   006.6′765   87-2024
ISBN 0 471 91501 7

British Library Cataloguing in Publication Data:
Ammeraal, L.
  Computer graphics for the IBM PC.
  1. Computer graphics   2. IBM Personal
  Computer—Programming
  I. Title
  006.6   T385
ISBN 0 471 91501 7

Printed and bound in Great Britain by The Universities Press (Belfast) Ltd.

Contents

Preface

In my earlier book *Programming Principles in Computer Graphics* I used the four primitive routines *initgr, move, draw, endgr,* and I assumed that anyone who wishes to use these routines on a particular computer could easily make them available. In computer graphics, we should distinguish at least two levels of abstraction, or, in other words, two software layers. At the lower level some convenient but elementary routines, such as those mentioned, are implemented, and at the higher level, they are simply used. In my earlier book on graphics I focussed on the higher level, and, frankly speaking, the lower level then seemed less interesting to me. When that book was printed, the publisher asked me to supply its programs on a diskette for the IBM PC, and doing so, I had to deal with that lower level as well. I observed that for many users of the IBM PC the question:

"How to obtain graphics output using the C language?"

is not trivial at all, and, in short, it became clear to me that the subject of 'raster graphics' is worth writing another book.

Some other books on computer graphics discuss the difference between 'vector graphics' and 'raster graphics' in rather abstract terms and with emphasis on hardware characteristics. From this, one might erroneously draw the conclusion that my 'vector-oriented' elementary routines should not be suitable for raster graphics devices such as a video display and a matrix printer. In my opinion, once we have decided to deal with the lower level of graphics, the best way to avoid such a misconception is to discuss concrete examples of both hardware and software.

The software presented and explained in this new book was written for the IBM PC and compatible machines using PC DOS or MS DOS, with either the usual color graphics adapter or a monochrome graphics adapter such as the well-known 'Hercules Card' from Hercules Computer Technology. Another technical point to be mentioned is that I used Lattice C, version 3.00G. I hope that the book will be instructive also for users of other compilers, or even of other hardware. After all, the C program text contains many rather simple routines, which could easily be modified, if necessary.

Some peculiarities of hardware and software discussed in the book will sooner or later be outdated, so one might wonder whether it can be used as a *textbook*. In teaching, we always have to distinguish between fundamental aspects and technical details. However, the former are best exemplified by the latter. Students are interested in a video display of $M \times N$ pixels only if we mention some concrete values of M and N. As teachers, we had better do this, even though such values will not be valid forever. In textbooks on microcomputers, technical details must be mentioned, and this book is not an exception to this. I hope that it will turn out to be useful in teaching practical computer science, both at universities and in polytechnic schools.

There are also many *professionals* who write programs to make a living. If they deal with graphics on an IBM PC or a compatible machine, then buying this book may save them money. They may either copy the graphics functions as they are listed, or use the underlying ideas for their own benefit. In particular, their attention will be drawn to the CAD program in Chapter 6.

Last but not least, the book might be interesting for the '*advanced hobbyist*'. These days a great many people use an IBM compatible PC at home, and, though a minority, a considerable number among them are familiar with some reasonable programming language, of which C is a good example. This book will show them that despite the absence of built-in graphics facilities, the C language is very suitable for obtaining graphics output.

L. Ammeraal

CHAPTER 1

Introduction

1.1. HISTORY AND SCOPE OF THIS BOOK

In my book *Programming Principles in Computer Graphics* (published by John Wiley, Chichester, 1986) I presented a number of programs, written in the C language, which used four primitive routines for graphics, namely:

initgr( )	to initialize graphics output;
move(x, y)	to move a (real or fictitious) pen to point (x, y);
draw(x, y)	to draw a line segment from the current position of the pen to point (x, y);
endgr( )	to perform any final actions.

It was easy for me to use these four functions on a PRIME 750, since I could express them into subroutines such as *PLOT,* available in DIPLOT, a device-independent plot library, well-known to many Fortran programmers who use CALCOMP plotters. Thanks to these subroutines, I could restrict myself to using them, not bothering about how they work internally. It makes sense to distinguish two software layers, or levels of abstraction. At the higher level we use device-independent routines, and at the lower level we implement them. Obviously, if such routines are available then the most practical thing to do is to use them, and this is why my earlier book was written at the higher level of abstraction.

Then why write a new book, which deals with the lower level? The simple answer to this question is that the primitive routines that people need are not always immediately available to them.

During the production process of my previous graphics book, the publisher asked me if I could deliver the programs listed in the book on a diskette to be used on the IBM Personal Computer and compatible machines. Somewhat embarrassed, I had to confess that though regarding myself as a computer professional, I had only occasionally used an IBM PC and was not sure that implementing my graphics programs on this machine would be a great success. (Incidentally, there are still many experienced programmers of main frame and mini computers who have not yet discovered the PC and who consequently will not appreciate this book; fortunately their number is decreasing.) Other IBM PC users told me that in the C language no handy primitive graphics functions such as I needed were available, and that I would have to write them myself. I realized, however, that it would be unwise to reject my publisher's request, so after some investigation I bought an IBM compatible PC, which, sooner or later, I would have done anyway. With some help from my publisher and other kind people, it was then relatively easy to implement the functions *initgr, move, draw, endgr,* and to make the programs of my earlier book run on the IBM PC.

1

Writing these four primitive functions turned out to be a nice low-level programming exercise, and there were so many people interested in it that I decided to extend the project somewhat and write a second graphics book about it. A separate treatment of high-level and low-level graphics programming in two books might be unusual, but it avoids the confusion of talking at two levels at the same time. In this low-level book, our first goal is to develop a tiny graphics package, which consists of only little more than the four primitive functions that I originally needed. If this is all you need, Chapters 1 and 2 will do. However, once we have decided to devote our attention to 'raster graphics', we also want to deal with its special features. For example, on the screen of a video display, drawn line segments can be erased, which is not possible with a pen plotter. This will be the subject of Chapter 3. In Chapter 4, we use matrix printers for graphics output. If you have such a printer, you will be able to produce a hard copy of your graphics results without buying a pen plotter. Chapter 5 deals with writing text in combination with graphics, and shows how to add special characters such as an integral sign. Finally, in Chapter 6 we shall develop a simple drawing system. Since this requires no special hardware, there are no obstacles to use it in practice, or, at least, to experiment with it. In general, the book encourages you to be active. It may disappoint you if you expect it to inform you about advanced research projects. Admiring achievements of others gives you less satisfaction than using your own brain, hands and PC.

1.2 SOME SPECIAL POINTS FOR THE C PROGRAMMER

I assume that you are familiar with the C language as it is presented in my book *C For Programmers*. As emphasized there, when using C on a specific machine with a specific compiler, we may need some additional information. We are now using the IBM PC or a compatible machine; the C programs and functions we are going to discuss were compiled with the Lattice C compiler, Version 3.0. If you use a different compiler, you should be aware of some special Lattice C characteristics, so that, if necessary, you can adapt the program text as required by your compiler. I shall therefore try to provide you with such information in the following subsections.

1.2.1 Type unsigned char

At various places you will notice the type *unsigned char*. In Lattice C, Version 3, the keyword *unsigned* before *char* prevents the leftmost bit of a character from being interpreted as a sign bit. Such a sign bit would be extended to the left if the character is converted to type *int*. For example, after

   unsigned char $k = 0xC0$; /* *In binary*: 1100 0000 */

the result of the right shift operation

$$k \gg 4$$

will be $0x0C$ $(=0 \ldots 0$ 1100, in binary) which in most applications is what we want. But if k were of type *char* (instead of *unsigned char*), the 'sign bit' 1 would be used to 'widen' 1100 0000 to 1111 1111 1100 0000, and this, shifted right four positions, would yield 0000 1111 1111 1100. Note that now the value of the rightmost eight bits is 0xFC. If this is undesirable, the keyword *unsigned* is a good remedy: it causes 1100 0000 to be widened to 0000 0000 1100 0000, which, after the right-shift, yields the correct value 0000 0000 0000 1100.

1.2.2 Direct input from the keyboard

We normally use the file pointer *stdin* for 'standard input' if we want to read something from the keyboard. For example,

scanf(*"%d"*, &*n*)   is equivalent to   *fscanf*(*stdin*, *"%d"*, &*n*), and
getchar( )   is equivalent to   *getc*(*stdin*).

These functions use a buffer, which implies that the characters we are typing are actually used only when we press the Enter key. This enables us to use the backspace key for corrections. Sometimes we wish the characters to be used the very moment we type them, without the obligation to press the Enter key. In Lattice C we have the following two functions for this purpose:

getch( )   Get a character from the keyboard, no echo.
getche( )   Get a character from the keyboard, echo.

Here 'echo' means that the character that we enter is displayed on the screen. With *getche* this happens in the same way as with *getchar*. We shall see that sometimes the machine is in 'graphics mode'; then echoing the entered character is not desired, so *getch* is suitable in that case.

Another useful non-standard function is

kbhit( )   Check if the keyboard is hit.

In contrast to normal input functions, *kbhit* will not wait until some key is pressed. It simply returns the value 1 if a key has been pressed, and 0 otherwise. If a character has been entered, *kbhit* will not skip over that character, in other words, the character can still be read in the normal way. The function *kbhit* enables us to terminate a loop when a key is pressed, as for example in

```
main()
{ int n=0; double x=1.0;
  while (1)
  { x *= 1.000000001; n++;
    if (kbhit()) break;
  }
  printf("n = %d   x = %f", n, x);
}
```

There is also a function *ungetch,* similar to the standard I/O function *ungetc.* We can use it after calling *getch* or *getche* to push a character onto a stack, so that it will be used when we call *getch* or *getche* again. The stack is only one level deep, so we should not push a second character onto it. In the example

```
ch1 = getch(); ungetch(ch1); ch2 = getch();
```

only one character will effectively be read from the keyboard, and this character is assigned to both *ch*1 and *ch*2. We shall use *ungetch* in subsection 1.2.4.

1.2.3 Memory models; peek and poke

The 8088/8086 processor employs a segmented addressing technique. Each address consists of two 16-bit components: a segment and an offset. The segment is shifted four bits to the left, that is, it is extended with four zero bits on the right-hand side, and then the offset is added to it. In this way we obtain a 20-bit address, sufficient for a 1-megabyte address space. There are four 'segment registers' to contain segments, namely

CS	'Code Segment'
DS	'Data Segment'
SS	'Stack Segment'
ES	'Extra Segment'

As long as our program fits into 64K bytes, it is possible to keep the segment constant in CS, and vary only the offset. Similarly, as long as our data area does not exceed 64K bytes, the segment in DS can be constant. In this way we use only 16-bit addresses, both for instruction fetching and for data access. This leads to more efficient code than when 20-bits addresses are used, and for a great many applications, a 64K program area and (another) 64K data area are sufficient. We call this way of using memory the S model (where S stands for Small). Besides the S model, we can use the P model if only the program size exceeds 64K, the D model if only the data exceeds 64K, or the L model (Large) if both program and data exceed 64K. We can specify to the compiler which model is desired; each model has its own library, so compiling and linking must be consistent wilth respect to the memory model. The default model is S, so this will be used if we do not tell the compiler anything about a model. We shall use this S model in all our programs; even the rather large drawing program to be discussed in Chapter 6 fits into 64K bytes.

The above discussion is rather machine-oriented; it could have been omitted if we had not to deal with graphics. However, in the next chapter, we shall directly access the graphics adapter, as if it were located in the normal memory, starting at address 0xB8000. Note that this is a 20-bit address, written in hexadecimal notation. We shall use the term 'screen memory' for the amount of memory located in the graphics adapter. It would be a pity if only for this special purpose we had to use the D or the L model. Fortunately, there are two functions in Lattice C to move data to and from such a memory area, respectively:

```
poke(segment, offset, source, nbytes)
peek(segment, offset, destination, nbytes)
```

For the first argument we use 0xB800. Note that this is only a 16-bit value, since, as mentioned above, it will be extended with four zero bits on the right-hand side. The first two arguments have type (unsigned) integer. The second argument is the offset to be used relative to the extended first argument. The third argument is a normal pointer to a character, so it may be the name of an array of characters. The fourth argument has type (unsigned) integer; it says how many bytes are to be copied.

1.2.4 Console break

We sometimes stop a running program using Ctrl Break, which means that we press the Break key while the Ctrl key is kept down. If there is no Break key, the combination Ctrl C is used for this purpose. Let us use the term 'console break' for either method. There are two kinds of problems with the console break, and especially for graphics programs it is important to solve them. The first problem is that the machine may not listen when we are trying to use the break facility. The operating system checks for a console break only on certain occasions. Depending on whether or not a 'break check flag' has been set, it performs this check either on any 'service request' or only on a console service request. If only computations are carried out, such as, for example, in the loop

```
for (i=0; i<30000; i++) s += 1 + 2 * (i / 2);
```

there is no such request, so the program will refuse to be interrupted by a console break. I actually encountered this problem in a more interesting computation than this one, and I then started looking for some innocent service request (preferably a console service request), which I could insert in the loop to make the operation system perform the desired check. I first tried a simple call of the function *kbhit* (see 1.2.2), which turned out to work satisfactorily in most situations. However, it did not work when I redundantly pressed some key before using the console break. This sometimes happens, for example, if only some letter should be entered, and we press not only the key with that letter, but also the Enter key. I therefore extended this solution, and used the following function:

```
checkbreak()
{ char ch;
  if (kbhit()) { ch = getch(); kbhit(); ungetch(ch); }
}
```

If *checkbreak* is called in the inner part of the above for-loop, the program will listen to our console break.

The second point is: What will happen if and when the machine listens to our console-break request? If we do not specify any action ourselves, the console break will activate the default interrupt handler, which simply stops program execution. In most programs this is what we want, but in graphics programs another action will be necessary, as we will see in Section 2.9. In general, we can 'plant a break trap' by writing a special function that says what should be done if and when a console break occurs. The address of that function, simply written as its name, is passed as an argument to the function *onbreak,* available in Lattice C. If our function returns a value of 0, the execution resumes at the interrupted point. Otherwise the program is aborted immediately. The function *onbreak* may also be given a null pointer as its argument; this may be written as the number 0. In that case the default interrupt handler will again be used when a console break occurs. If the argument of *onbreak* is not 0 but a function, it should be declared as such before it is used, otherwise the compiler would mistake it for a simple integer variable. Here is a demonstration of all this. It is based on the program in Subsection 1.2.2. Instead of pressing any key, we now use a normal console break.

```
/* BREAKDEMO.C: Console-break demonstration */
#include "dos.h"
int n=0, my_function();
double x=1.0;

main()
{ onbreak(my_function); /* Replace default interrupt handler */
  while (n<30000)         /* with  my_function.                */
  { x *= 1.000000001; n++;
    checkbreak();
  }
  onbreak(0);
  /* Any program text inserted here, when interrupted, would
     invoke the default interrupt handler.                    */
  printf("Normal program end, n = 30000   x = %f", x);
}

int my_function()
{ printf("n = %d    x = %f", n, x);
  exit(0);
}

checkbreak()
{ char ch;
  if (kbhit()) { ch = getch(); kbhit(); ungetch(ch); }
}
```

Note that *my_function* calls the standard function *exit*. It does not return to the main program, so it need not contain a return statement specifying whether or not the program is to resume, as mentioned above.

As a final remark we note that on an IBM PC there is a subtle difference between Ctrl Break and Ctrl C. If we run *BREAKDEMO.C* and we redundantly press any key more than once prior to a console break, Ctrl Break works properly but Ctrl C has no effect. If we press such a key only once or not at all before the console break, which is more likely, Ctrl Break and Ctrl C have identical effects.

1.2.5   Accessing the 8088 I/O ports

The lowest level at which input and output can be programmed is based on the elementary machine instructions *IN* and *OUT*. These instructions are normally used only by assembly-language programmers (and even for them higher-level I/O facilities are available, as Subsection 1.2.6 will show). The instruction *IN* reads data from an input port, and *OUT* writes data to an output port. These I/O ports are special hardware circuits used by the computer to communicate with external devices. All high-level routines for input and output eventually result in the execution of *IN* and *OUT* instructions. These instructions are also available in Lattice C. They are used as follows

```
v = inp(p);
outp(p, v);
```

where p and v have type (unsigned) int, p being the port address and v the port value. When using the functions *inp* and *outp*, we have to use the line

```
#include "dos.h"
```

in our program.

Direct accessing I/O ports incorrectly may cause all sorts of system problems, so it is strongly advised to use higher level I/O functions instead, wherever possible. The software in this book will not directly access I/O ports if it is running on a machine with a color graphics adapter. With a Hercules card (or a compatible monochrone graphics adapter), however, it will use the function *outp* to switch from text mode to graphics mode, and vice versa.

1.2.6 Registers and software interrupts

We shall now see how the computer can communicate with the outside world at a higher level than with directly accessing I/O ports. There is a set of routines, called Basic Input and Output System, or, briefly, *BIOS*. You will not expect that switching to a higher level requires more knowledge of the machine architecture, but curiously enough, to some extent this is the case. We cannot possibly use BIOS routines unless we know some general registers of the 8088 (or 8086) processor. We can understand this if we realize that these routines were designed to be called in assembly-language programs, not in a high-level language such as C. We need not discuss the entire 8088 register set, but we can restrict ourselves to the four Data Registers, shown in Fig. 1.1.

AX	AH	AL	Accumulator
BX	BH	BL	Base
CX	CH	CL	Count
DX	DH	DL	Data

Fig. 1.1. 8088 Data Registers

Each of the registers AX, BX, CX, DX contains 16 bits. It is divided into a high-order and a low-order byte, each of which can be used as an eight-bit register. For example, if FA3B (hex.) is loaded in DX, the contents of DH and DL will be FA and 3B, respectively.

Another rather technical aspect is the way BIOS routines are called. A BIOS routine is not called as a subroutine, but as a so-called 'software interrupt'. This term is derived from the interrupt mechanism that is used for signals from the outside world. A running program is then really interrupted, but in such a way that normal program execution can be resumed later. When such an interrupt occurs, all register contents are pushed onto a stack, and a jump takes place to a location whose address is obtained from a table, the so-called interrupt vector. The program fragment starting at that location is called an interrupt routine. It ends with the instruction 'Return from Interrupt', which takes care that the saved register contents are popped from the stack, and that the execution of the interrupted program is resumed. In the same way as by external interrupts, our program can be 'interrupted' by a special instruction, called a software interrupt. Since the programmer decides where a software interrupt is to take place, it is conceptually similar to a subroutine call, but its implementation is similar to the way external interrupts are dealt with. Instead of the address of a subroutine, we only need a (usually small) number to identify the software interrupt. For all software interrupts associated with the video display, this number is 16, usually written hexadecimally as 10. In an assembly-language program we use the instruction

```
INT 10H
```

to initiate any video software interrupt. Since interrupt 10H is used for many purposes, we have to use some parameter-passing mechanism. This is why we need the data registers of Fig. 1.1 in this context. Using Lattice C, we can write

```
int86(0x10, &regsin, &regsout);
```

The first argument is the interrupt number 10H. The second and the third arguments are the addresses of data structures which correspond to the registers that we would use in an equivalent assembly-language program. Any information to be passed to the routine is to be supplied in *regsin*, and any information returned by the routine will be available through *regsout*. To use all this, we have to write

```
#include "dos.h"
```

and to declare

```
union REGS regsin, regsout;
```

In the header file *dos.h*, the type *union REGS* is defined as in the third of the following three lines:

```
struct XREG { short ax,bx,cx,dx,si,di; };
struct HREG { byte al,ah,bl,bh,cl,ch,dl,dh; };
union REGS { struct XREG x; struct HREG h; };
```

In an object of type *union REGS*, the structures *x* and *h* occupy the same memory, which is just what we want. For example, *regsin.x.ax* shares memory with both *regsin.h.ah* and *regsin.h.al*, in the same way as the two-bytes register AX is divided into the two one-byte registers AH and AL, and so on. (Please, do not worry about *si* and *di* in the first of the above three lines or about the order in which *al* and *ah* occur in the second: I would rather not discuss the 8088 processor in more detail at this moment.) Before the software interrupt (number 10H) takes place, we have to place an unique code into register AH. In C, we achieve this as follows:

```
regsin.h.ah = code;
int86(0x10, &regsin, &regsout);
```

This code tells the interrupt routine which of several possible actions is required. For our purposes, there will be no need for two distinct arguments *regsin* and *regsout*: the same structure *regs* can be used for both purposes, so we will simply declare

```
union REGS regs;
```

and use *regs* instead of both *regsin* and *regsout*. Besides AH, some of the other registers may have to be filled to specify what we want in more detail, as we will see in Section 2.3.

1.2.7 The maximum stack size

Automatic variables and return addresses of functions are placed on a stack, which is a contiguous piece of memory. There is a default limitation imposed on the stack size, which may be insufficient, especially if we use recursive functions. Lattice C offers the possibility to choose a maximum stacksize larger than the default value. All we have to do is to write, for example,

```
unsigned int  _STACK = 15000;
main()
{ ...
  ...
}
```

if we want the value 15000 to override the default value (of 2048). The size may now be as large as 15000 bytes.

Incidentally, we can in turn override that new value when we give the command to execute the program. For example, if our program is called *MYPROG.EXE*, we can specify that the stack size limit is to be 20000 bytes by entering the command

```
MYPROG =20000
```

Since we assume that our programs will also be used by people who are not interested in such implementation details as stack sizes, we prefer the former method of specifying the maximum stacksize. If, in this example, the value 20000 is used for *_STACK* in the program text, then the user can simply enter the command

```
MYPROG
```

with the same effect as the more extensive *MYPROG* command above.

1.3 GRAPHICS ADAPTERS

On the screen of our video display, there are a great many points, and each of them can be made light or dark, or, as we sometimes say, white or black. The screen may be able to display colors, but we shall not deal with other colors than white and black. These white or black points are called picture elements, abbreviated as *pixels* or sometimes *pels*. The more pixels there are, the higher the resolution. The *graphics adapter,* also called *board,* or *card,* is the piece of hardware which determines this resolution. The three most popular graphics adapters, with their characteristics, are:

- Monochrome display adapter, used for text only; it displays 25 lines of 80 characters each.
- Monochrome graphics adapter (such as a Hercules Card), used both for text and graphics.
  When used for text, it is identical with the monochrome display adapter.
  When used for graphics, it has 720×348 pixels (348 lines of 720 pixels each).
- Color graphics adapter, used either for text or for graphics.
  When used for text, it displays 25×80 characters.
  When used for graphics, it has 640×200 pixels (or less if other colors than white and black are used).

  These adapters contain memory, which we can address in the usual way. We can display text or graphics by placing appropriate data in this area of memory. However, the way data is coded for text is essentially different from the way it is coded for graphics. For text, the ASCII value of each character to be displayed is stored in one byte, followed by a so-called attribute byte which contains information about how the character is to be displayed. (For example, there is an attribute to underline characters.) The transformation of these two bytes into a pixel pattern is performed by a special piece of hardware, called a *character generator*. This provides an efficient way of displaying characters. We have $25 \times 80 = 2000$ character positions on the screen, and as each character is coded in two bytes, we need 4000 bytes. This number if very low if we realize that each character is represented on the screen in a box of 9×14 pixels (14 horizontal lines of 9 pixels each). If for each pixel one bit were needed, this would take $2000 \times 14 \times 9/8 = 31500$ bytes. The addresses of the 4000 bytes actually used are B0000, . . . , B0F9F. The important thing to remember is that, when using the *monochrome display adapter,* we cannot suppress the activity of the character generator. This is why the monochrome display adapter cannot reasonably be used for graphics. Note that its name does not include the term *graphics* as with the other two adapters.

The *monochrome graphics adapter* is a most ingenious device. (Incidentally, it should not be confused with the monochrome display adapter mentioned above; the frequently used term 'Hercules card' avoids such confusion, but that term is correct only if the adapter was made by Hercules Computer Technology, which may not be the case.) First of all, the monochrome graphics adapter can be used to generate characters in exactly the same way as the monochrome display adapter. However, with the monochrome graphics adapter we can suppress the activity of the character generator, and switch from 'text mode' to the 'graphics mode' (also called 'bit-mapped mode'). In graphics mode, each pixel corresponds to one bit in memory. If the bit is 1, the corresponding pixel is lit, if it is 0, the pixel is dark. There are 720 pixels on a horizontal line, which corresponds to $720/8 = 90$ bytes. As there are 348 lines, the amount of memory needed is $348 \times 90 = 31320$, which is rounded up to $32K = 32768$ bytes. In hexadecimal notation, the addresses B0000, . . . , B7FFF are used for this purpose. Besides, the monochrome graphics adapter has another 'page' of 32K, with the addresses B8000, . . . , BFFFF. We can use both pages, but at each moment only one of them is displayed. If we use only one we can freely choose either of them. The pages starting at the addresses B0000 and B8000 are numbered 0, 1, respectively. We shall use page 1 for two reasons. First, its begin address B8000 is the same as for the color graphics adapter, as we shall see presently, so we can now always use the same begin address. Second, page 0 overlaps the text display memory, and page 1 does not. So if something valuable is in page 1, it remains unaffected if we switch to text mode. In Chapter 4, we shall use this to produce a 'post-mortem' graphics screen dump.

The *color graphics adapter* is needed if we want pictures in various colors. Like the monochrome graphics adapter, this adapter can operate either in text mode or in a bit-mapped graphics mode. Yet I would recommend it only if colors are really needed, since it has three drawbacks:

1. It generates character patterns in a 8×8 box instead of in a 9×14 box as with the other two adapters. This reduces the readability considerably.

2. In text mode, the screen blinks when the display scrolls, which is somewhat irritating.
3. In graphics mode, it has a comparatively low resolution, namely at most 640×200. There are in fact three bit-mapped modes for this adapter

640×200 monochrome (called 'high resolution')
320×200 4 colors
160×100 16 colors

In the 640×200 resolution, we need $640 \times 200/8 = 16000$ bytes. This is rounded up to 16K; the addresses are B8000, . . . , BBFFF.

If you think of buying a graphics adapter or a complete PC, you have to choose between the monochrome graphics adapter and the color graphics adapter (or buy them both!). Obviously, if colors are essential, you need the color graphics adapter. If not, the monochrome graphics adapter seems to be a better choice. There is, however, another point which should not be overlooked, namely which of either adapter can be used in combination with the software you are going to use. I am not familiar enough with commercially available packages to give you any general advice on this point. Since it was IBM's choice, the BIOS Video routines in PC DOS were written for the color graphics adapter, not for the monochrome graphics adapter. This means that when we are programming for the monochrome graphics adapter, we have to work at a lower level than for the color graphics adapter. In the first case we have to use direct access to screen memory and to I/O ports, instead of delegating this to BIOS routines. This seems a greater disadvantage of the monochrome graphics adapter than it really is. For the color graphics adapter we can use either method, as we shall see in Chapter 2, but even here I prefer the direct method of writing into screen memory. For some applications, where speed is at stake, it may be desirable to program some routines in assembly language and to bypass the BIOS routines when updating the screen, since for such applications these are rather slow. However, we use the C language and the BIOS routines were written in assembly language, so I do not claim that in our case the direct method is faster then the BIOS routines. But is is reasonably fast, and by using C, we see more clearly what is going on than by using assembly language. In a later stage, we could rewrite the most frequently used C function (called *dot*) in assembly language to speed it up, and then it is nice that the C program text already uses the direct method and can therefore be translated literally.

Note that these low-level and device-dependent aspects concern only (a minor part of) the module which contains our four primitive graphics functions *initgr, move, draw* and *endgr,* so the user of these functions need not worry about I/O ports or BIOS routines.

Initially, I developed two versions of that module, one for either graphics adapter, and the user had to choose the one he needed. However, I realized later than only one will do if we let the machine make such a choice. In this way, we can write truly portable graphics software, in that the executable version of a program can be used on an IBM (compatible) PC, regardless whether the PC has a color graphics or a monochrome graphics adapter. In Chapter 2 we shall develop such a generalized module.

CHAPTER 2

Line drawing

2.1 SCREEN AND PIXEL COORDINATES

In most applications it is convenient if one unit of length in the horizontal direction has the same real size as one unit in the vertical direction. We shall therefore use a coordinate system with coordinates x and y, and one unit in either direction will be about one inch. As usual in mathematics, the x- and the y-axis will point to the right and upward, respectively, and we shall place the origin in the bottom-left corner of the screen. It is nice to know the maximum values that we may use for either coordinate, and, instead of using the exact dimensions of the screen of my monitor (which may be different on other monitors), I chose the round numbers 10 and 7 for these maximum values. These numbers are easy to remember, and their proportion is a reasonable approximation of the ratio between the two dimensions of most screens. For our convenience, we shall use the term 'inch' for our unit of length, which is strictly correct only if our monitor has a screen of exactly 10×7 inches. In our program text the numbers 10.0 and 7.0 occur only once, namely in the definitions $x\_max = 10.0$ and $y\_max = 7.0$. Everywhere else we use x_max and y_max to denote these numbers.

$$0 \leqq x \leqq x\_max \qquad (x\_max = 10.0)$$
$$0 \leqq y \leqq y\_max \qquad (y\_max = 7.0)$$

These coordinates are real numbers, hence the notation 10.0 and 7.0 instead of 10 and 7.

We shall also use pixel coordinates. These are integers and we shall use capital letters X and Y for them. We shall write their maximum values as $X\_\_max$ and $Y\_\_max$. Note the double underscore $\_\_$; it provides another distinction between the notations for screen and pixel coordinates.

$$0 \leqq X \leqq X\_\_max \qquad (X\_\_max \text{ is equal to either 719 or 639})$$
$$0 \leqq Y \leqq Y\_\_max \qquad (Y\_\_max \text{ is equal to either 347 or 199})$$

The Y-axis points downward, so the origin $(X, Y) = (0, 0)$ of the pixel coordinate system lies in the top-left corner of the screen. This is why the conversion from y to Y involves a subtraction, not present in the conversion from x to X. In the C language we define the following functions for the two conversions:

```
int IX(x) float x; { return (int)(x*horfact+0.5); }
int IY(y) float y; { return Y__max-(int)(y*vertfact+0.5); }
```

where *horfact* and *vertfact* are multiplication factors which in *initgr* are computed as follows:

```
horfact  = X__max/x_max;
vertfact = Y__max/y_max;
```

Remember that the cast-operator consisting of the keyword *int* surrounded by parentheses truncates its operand. Thus adding 0.5 to some nonnegative value before truncating causes that value to be rounded to the nearest integer. We check this operation for the extreme values of x and y:

```
IX(0.0)   = (int) (0.0 * X__max / x_max + 0.5) = 0
IX(x_max) = (int)(x_max * X__max / x_max + 0.5) = X__max

IY(0.0)   = Y__max - (int)(0.0 * Y__max / y_max + 0.5) = Y__max
IY(y_max) = Y__max - (int)(y_max * Y__max / y_max + 0.5) = 0
```

The functions *IX* and *IY* are extremely useful, since they convert the given screen coordinates x and y, used at the higher user level, into the pixel coordinates X and Y which at the lower level, where we deal with graphics adapters, are needed.

The functions *move* and *draw*, used throughout my book *Programming Principles in Computer Graphics*, assume the existence of a *current pen position*. We shall denote this position by the global variables $X1$ and $Y1$, which are its pixel coordinates. These variables are integers; especially on microcomputers, where normally no floating-point hardware is available, it is important to use integers wherever this is possible. We shall use the keyword *static* for these and some other variables. This implies that they can be used only in the file where they are defined. A complete set of graphics functions and variable definitions will reside in one file (or module), as we shall see in Section 2.10. All these functions have access to (external) static variables such as $X1$ and $Y1$, but a user's program has not, so it cannot inadvertently destroy their values. Function *move* mainly consists of statements to update the current pen position, or, as we sometimes say, 'the current point':

```
static int X1, Y1;

move(x, y) double x, y;
{ X1 = IX(x); Y1 = IY(y); check(X1, Y1);
}
```

The definition of the function *check* will be shown later. As you may have guessed, its task is to test whether the point given by the arguments $X1$, $Y1$ lies within the screen boundaries. For x and y we have used type *double* instead of *float*. This does not imply that high precision is essential here, but float arguments are always converted to double in C, so even if we had written *float x, y*, the parameters x and y would have been of type double.

We now turn to the most interesting one of our four primitive functions, namely *draw*. Recall that its task is to draw a line segment from the current pen position to a new point (x, y). Thus the starting point of the line segment is given by the global integer variables $X1$, $Y1$, and the end point by the floating parameters x, y. It would be nicer to deal with (integer) pixel coordinates for both points and to have both points available as function parameters. We therefore introduce a new function, *draw_line*, which does nearly all the work. This important function will be the subject of Section 2.2, but we use it here already. Function *draw* can now be written as follows:

```
draw(x, y) double x, y;
{ int X2, Y2;
  X2 = IX(x); Y2 = IY(y); check(X2, Y2);
  draw_line(X1, Y1, X2, Y2);
  X1 = X2; Y1 = Y2;
}
```

2.2 LINE DRAWING WITH INTEGER ARITHMETIC

The function *draw_line* remains to be implemented. Since speed is at stake here, the final version of this function will be rather sophisticated, and, without any explanations, probably hard to understand. We shall therefore discuss several versions, each version being a refinement of its predecessor. In a slightly different form, the algorithm under consideration was published by Bresenham in 1965.

Between the points $(X1, Y1)$ and $(X2, Y2)$, supplied to *draw_line* as arguments, usually a great many points are to be computed. Let us assume that for each of these intermediate points (X, Y) we can write a dot on the screen by the function call

```
dot(X, Y);
```

The implementation of this low-level function *dot* depends on the graphics adapter that we are using, so we shall discuss that subject in the Sections 2.4 and 2.5. Our present task is to find out which grid points (X, Y) of the screen are to be used. Since there are so many of these points to be computed, we shall eventually use only integer arithmetic, which is considerably faster than floating-point computations. However, in our first version we shall ignore this aspect for reasons of simplicity. It gives good results only in the case that the position of P2 $(X2, Y2)$ relative to P1 $(X1, Y1)$ is roughly as indicated in Fig. 2.1.

P2
X

P1
X

Fig. 2.1. Position of P2 relative to P1

Moving from P1 to P2, we are going to the right and possibly upward, but the vertical distance between the points P1 and P2 is at most equal to their horizontal distance, in other words:

$$X1 \ < \ X2$$
$$Y1 \ \leqq \ Y2$$
$$Y2 - Y1 \leqq X2 - X1$$

(In accordance with normal mathematical usage, we let the Y-axis point upward, temporarily ignoring the fact that the actual Y-axis points downward, as this is irrelevant to our present discussion.) Our first version of *draw_line* can now be written:

```
draw_line1(X1, Y1, X2, Y2) int X1, Y1, X2, Y2;
{ float t; int X, Y;
  t = (float)(Y2-Y1)/(float)(X2-X1);
  for (X = X1; X <= X2; X++)
  { Y = Y1 + (int)(t * (X-X1) + 0.5);
    dot(X, Y);
  }
}
```

For the general case, without the restriction mentioned above, we have to investigate which of the variables X and Y is the independent one, controlled by the for loop. Of course, we choose that one which corresponds to the greater of the absolute differences $|Y2 - Y1|$ and $|X2 - X1|$. Furthermore, the controlled variable may have to be decremented instead of incremented, and if $t*(X - X1)$ is negative it should be decreased by 0.5 (rather than increased) before truncating it to an integer. We shall not dwell upon all these details, since that would not lead to a practical function anyway. It is more interesting to improve the function in quite another direction, namely by replacing floating with integer arithmetic. If I gave the final version at once, it would be hard to understand, so we had better increase the level of complexity by small steps. For the moment we shall again assume that the position of P2 relative to P1 is as shown in Fig. 2.1. For that case we will now develop an algorithm which still uses floating variables, but in such a way that these can easily be eliminated, as we shall see. Consider, for example, Fig. 2.2, with the given points P1 $(1, 1)$ and P2 $(12, 5)$. (Thus $X1 = 1$, $Y1 = 1$, $X2 = 12$, $Y2 = 5$.)

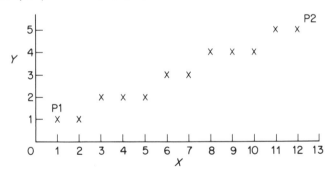

Fig. 2.2. P1, P2 and intermediate points

To find the points between P1 and P2, as shown in Fig. 2.2, we proceed as follows. Initially we set $X = X1$ and $Y = Y1$. In a loop we increment X by one, and we either leave Y unchanged or increment it by one as well. Of course, the latter choice has to be made in such a way that the new grid point (X, Y) should lie as close to the line through P1 and P2 as possible. This means that the vertically measured distance between each newly selected point and that line must not be greater than 0.5. We introduce the variable d for this distance:

$$d = Yexact - Ygridpoint$$

and require that

$$-0.5 < d \leqq 0.5$$

The latter inequality provides us with a method to determine whether or not Y is to be incremented, as the following function shows:

```
draw_line2(X1, Y1, X2, Y2) int X1, Y1, X2, Y2;
{ int X, Y;
  float t, /* slope */
        d; /* deviation */
  t = (float)(Y2-Y1)/(float)(X2-X1);
  d = 0;
  Y = Y1;
  for (X = X1; X <= X2; X++)
  { dot(X, Y);
    d += t;
    if (d > 0.5){ Y++; d--; }
  }
}
```

The deviation d, as defined above, is initially set to zero, and is updated each time in the loop. Since d denotes how far the selected point lies below the exact line, it increases by the slope t if X is increased by one and if Y remains unchanged. This is not correct if d exceeds the value 0.5. In that case it is time to increase Y by one. Obviously, the deviation d ($= Yexact - Y$) should then be decreased by one. Thus we see that the variable d is an excellent means to decide whether or not Y is to be incremented.

We now wish to eliminate the floating variables t and d. We observe that the exact value of t in the mathematical sense is a rational number, since we have

$$t = \frac{Y2 - Y1}{X2 - X1}$$

where the numerator and the denominator are integers. Also, d is computed as a finite sum of terms, each equal to either t or -1, so d is a rational number as well, and, like t, can be written as a fraction with denominator $X2 - X1$. This means that we can simply switch to the integer variables T and D obtained by multiplying t and d by the denominator $X2 - X1$. We also wish to get rid of the noninteger constant 0.5. This is not difficult either, since all we need is an extra factor 2 in that denominator. Thus we use:

$$T = denom \cdot t$$
$$D = denom \cdot d$$

where

$$denom = 2(X2 - X1).$$

The if-statement in *draw_line2* could then be replaced with

```
if (D > dX) { Y++; D -= denom; }
```

where

$$dX = X2 - X1.$$

A computer can faster compare a quantity with zero than with a nonzero value such as dX. We therefore introduce the variable

$$E = D - dX$$

so that we can replace the condition $D > dX$ with $E > 0$. Of course, the initial value of E is $-dX$, which corresponds to $D = 0$. This leads to the improved function *draw_line3*:

```
draw_line3(X1, Y1, X2, Y2) int X1, Y1, X2, Y2;
{ int X, Y, T, E, dX, dY, denom;
  dX = X2 - X1;
  dY = Y2 - Y1;
  denom = dX << 1;    /* denom = 2 * dX  */
  T = dY << 1;        /*   T   = 2 * dY  */
  E = -dX;
  Y = Y1;
  for (X = X1; X <= X2; X++)
  { dot(X, Y);
    E += T;
    if (E > 0) { Y++; E -= denom; }
  }
}
```

Since this function uses only integers, the machine will perform the computation more rapidly, and so will we ourselves! The latter is not very important, but it is instructive to apply *draw_line3* to the example of Fig. 2.2. If we do this, we easily obtain Table 2.1, which shows the values of X, Y, and E as they are updated in each step. The heading of this table shows C-statements copied from function *draw_line3*. In each step, the numeric values in the table are valid immediately after the execution of the respective statement. Before the loop starts, we have:

$$dX = 11, \quad dY = 4, \quad denom = 22, \quad T = 8, \quad E = -11, \quad Y = 1.$$

Note that the Y-coordinates in the second column are indeed the integers that would be obtained by rounding the values *Yexact*, shown in the rightmost column. Thus we have obtained a fast algorithm to draw the line segment that connects the points P1 and P2, provided the position of P2 relative to P1 is as shown in Fig. 2.1.

The only thing that remains is to generalize *draw_line3* to our final function

Table 2.1 Successive values of X, Y, E computed by *draw_line3*, applied to the example of Fig. 2.2

dot(X, Y);		E+=T;	Y++;	E-=denom;	
X	Y	E	Y	E	Yexact
1	1	-3			1
2	1	5	2	-17	$1 + 4/11$
3	2	-9			$1 + 8/11$
4	2	-1			$2 + 1/11$
5	2	7	3	-15	$2 + 5/11$
6	3	-7			$2 + 9/11$
7	3	1	4	-21	$3 + 2/11$
8	4	-13			$3 + 6/11$
9	4	-5			$3 + 10/11$
10	4	3	5	-19	$4 + 3/11$
11	5	-11			$4 + 7/11$
12	5	-3			5

draw_line, which should accept any two points P1 and P2. We introduce the
variable *vertlonger,* which will indicate whether the vertical distance between P1 and
P2 is greater than the horizontal distance between them. If so, *Y* is to be the
independent variable instead of *X.* We shall use a while statement instead of a for
statement, so that within the loop we can test the variable *vertlonger* to decide
whether *Y* or *X* is to be incremented as an independent variable (similar to the
controlled variable in a for loop). The other variable is then the dependent variable:
it depends on the condition $E > 0$ whether or not it is incremented.

```
draw_line(X1, Y1, X2, Y2) int X1, Y1, X2, Y2;
{ int X, Y, T, E, dX, dY, denom, Xinc = 1, Yinc = 1,
  vertlonger = 0, aux;
  dX = X2 - X1; dY = Y2 - Y1;
  if (dX < 0) {Xinc = -1; dX = -dX;}
  if (dY < 0) {Yinc = -1; dY = -dY;}
  if (dY > dX) { vertlonger = 1; aux = dX; dX = dY; dY = aux; }
  denom = dX << 1;
  T = dY << 1;
  E = -dX; X = X1;
  Y = Y1;
  while (dX-- >= 0)
  { dot(X, Y);
    if ((E += T) > 0)
    { if (vertlonger) X += Xinc; else Y += Yinc;
      E -= denom;
    }
    if (vertlonger) Y += Yinc; else X += Xinc;
  }
}
```

2.3 USING INTERRUPT 10H TO LIGHT PIXELS

In Section 1.3 we have seen that graphics adapters contain a considerable amount of
memory, which we briefly call *screen memory.* A call of our function *dot* will
eventually cause one bit somewhere in screen memory to be set. There are several
ways to achieve this. One way is to use the service offered by the BIOS routines of
the operating system. We then use the concept of a 'software interrupt', as discussed
in Section 1.2. According to some people, it is the only neat way of accessing screen
memory, but it applies only to the color graphics adapter, so in Section 2.4 we shall
use a more general method, which I consider neat as well.

For the color graphics adapter we can use the following lines of program text:

```
#include "dos.h"
union REGS regs;

dot(X, Y) int X, Y;     /* Preliminary version, using BIOS */
{ regs.h.ah = 12;                /* code to light a pixel   */
  regs.h.al = 1;                 /* color code              */
  regs.x.cx = X;                 /* X coordinate            */
  regs.x.dx = Y;                 /* Y coordinate            */
  int86(0x10, &regs, &regs);     /* software interrupt 10H  */
}
```

Thus we use software interrupt 10H, with code 12, which says that the pixel with coordinates X and Y is to be lit. We have to place appropriate values into the machine registers AH, AL, CX, DX, as explained in the above comments. The notation for registers we use here was discussed in Section 1.2.

2.4 IMMEDIATE ACCESS TO SCREEN MEMORY

We can bypass the BIOS routine used in Section 2.3, and write directly into screen memory. If we programmed in assembly language, the method of this section would have been faster than what we did in Section 2.3, but now that we are programming in C, it is doubtful whether we can use the argument of efficiency. Anyway, we cannot implement the function *dot* with software interrupt 10H for the monochrome graphics adapter, so we really have to access screen memory ourselves, unless we use a color graphics adapter. For reasons of symmetry, we shall use the new method in that case as well, but let us deal with the monochrome graphics adapter first. As we know, the call *dot*(X, Y) means that the bit that corresponds to the pixel coordinates X, Y is to be set.

We begin with a simple example. Let us implement the call

```
dot(0, 0);
```

which means that the pixel in the top-left corner of the screen is to be set. We shall use the graphics page which starts at address B8000, so bit 7 (the leftmost bit) of the contents of that address is to be set. Of course, the other bits in this location must not be altered. Here the bitwise OR-operator combined with assignment, that is, the 'update operator' |=, is extremely useful, and so are the functions *peek* and *poke*, discussed in Section 1.2. We use *peek* to 'read from' screen memory, whereas *poke* 'writes into' screen memory. We need them both here:

```
char ch;
...
peek(0xB800, 0, &ch, 1);
   /* the contents of address B8000 are assigned to ch */

ch |= 0x80;
   /* leftmost bit of ch is set  */

poke(0xB800, 0, &ch, 1);
   /* the value of ch is placed into memory location B8000 */
```

Recall that each line of the screen consists of 720 pixels, which corresponds to 90 bytes. We would therefore expect the first byte for line Y to have address $0xB8000 + 90*Y$. However, for reasons related to raster-scan hardware, the address of that byte is

```
0xB8000 + 0x2000 * (Y % 4) + 90 * (Y / 4)
```

(Recall that in C we use the operators / and % to compute the quotient and the remainder of integer division.) Thus we have the following offsets (relative to

B8000):

Line number Y	Offset for leftmost point on line Y (relative to 0xB8000)
0	0
1	0x2000
2	0x4000
3	0x6000
4	90
5	0x2000 + 90
6	0x4000 + 90
7	0x6000 + 90
⋮	⋮
344	7740
345	02000 + 7740
346	04000 + 7740
347	06000 + 7740

Each of these starting positions corresponds to a point $(0, Y)$. We have to add the value in C computed as $X / 8$ to it in order to obtain the address of the byte in which the bit for point(X, Y) is located. The remainder $X \% 8$ is used to find the required bit position of within that byte. Since $X = 0$ should yield the leftmost bit, that is, bit 7, the correct bit number is found as $7 - X \% 8$. Thus we can implement $dot(X, Y)$ as follows:

```
/* This is a preliminary version of the function  dot;
   it works only for the monochrome graphics adapter */

dot(X, Y) int X, Y;
{ int offset;
  char ch;
  offset= 0x2000*(Y%4) + 90*(Y/4) + (X/8);
  peek(0xB800, offset, &ch, 1);
  ch |= 1 << (7-X%8);
  poke(0xB800, offset, &ch, 1);
}
```

Instead of

```
X / 8            X % 8           Y / 4           Y % 4
```

we shall actually use

```
X >> 3           X & 7           Y >> 2           Y & 3
```

The operators $\gg$ (shift right) and & (bitwise and) will probably be faster than / and %, and give the same results here, as can be seen by writing all operands in binary notation. In this way the second last statement of function dot would now read:

```
ch |= 1 << (7 - (X&7));
```

We can, however, replace this with the still faster statement

```
ch |= 0x80 >> (X&7);
```

since instead of using 0000 0001, shifting the 1-bit 7-($X\&7$) positions to the left, we may use 1000 0000 and shift the 1-bit $X\&7$ posiltions to the right. Thus we obtain the following function:

```
/* This is an improved version of the function  dot;
   it works only for the monochrome graphics adapter */

dot(X, Y) int X, Y;
{ int offset;
  char ch;
  offset= 0x2000 * (Y&3) + 90*(Y>>2) + (X>>3);
  peek(0xB800, offset, &ch, 1);
  ch |= 0x80 >> (X&7);
  poke(0xB800, offset, &ch, 1);
}
```

So much for the monochrome graphics adapter. We could now end this section, since for the color graphics adapter we have already implemented *dot* in a 'neat' way in Section 2.3, and why give two solutions if we need only one? One reason is that we want a single function *dot* for both adapters, and, though possible, using two essentially different methods in one function is not particularly elegant. Furthermore, we shall extend our set of functions later, and then things will be simpler with a consistent approach for the two adapter types. Recall that we already discussed this point nearly at the end of Chapter 1. In contrast to the function *dot* in Section 2.3, the following version shows what actually happens in screen memory:

```
/* This is another version of the function dot; it
   works only for the color graphics adapter, and can
   replace the version of this function listed in Section 2.3 */

dot(X, Y) int X, Y;
{ int offset;
  char ch;
  offset = 0x2000 * (Y&1) + 80 * (Y>>1) + (X>>3);
  peek(0xB800, offset, &ch, 1);
  ch |= 0x80 >> (X&7);
  poke(0xB800, offset, &ch, 1);
}
```

This version is similar to our last one for the monochrome graphics adapter. There the screen memory consisted of four partitions of 8KB each (8KB = 0x2000). Here we have two partitions of that size, the first for the lines $0, 2, \ldots, 198$, and the second for the lines $1, 3, \ldots, 199$. Thus we now have :

Line number Y	Offset for leftmost point on line Y (relative to 0xB8000)
0	0
1	0x2000
2	80
3	0x2000 + 80
4	160
5	0x2000 + 160
⋮	⋮
198	7920
199	0x2000 + 7920

The last two versions of the function *dot* differ only in some constants. Combining these two functions into one can now easily be accomplished by using variables instead of these constants, provided that we are able to assign the correct values to these variables before the function is called. We shall deal with this in the next section.

2.5 FINDING OUT THE ADAPTER TYPE

It would be awkward if for all low-level operations we had to discuss one version for either adapter. In particular, we want a single function *dot* for both graphics adapters. Such a more uniform approach is possible by using certain variables whose values depend on the adapter in use. The variables $X\_\_max$ and $Y\_\_max$, introduced in Section 2.1, are already examples of such variables. (As they will never change for one adapter, they can be regarded as constants, but we shall see that they can be determined at execution time, hence the term 'variables'). Similar to these two variables, we now introduce the 'variables' $c1$, $c2$ and $c3$, whose values, along with those of $X\_\_max$ and $Y\_\_max$ are listed in the following table

	Monochrome graphics adapter	Color graphics adapter
$X\_\_max$	719	639
$Y\_\_max$	347	199
$c1$	3	1
$c2$	90	80
$c3$	2	1

If we can use $c1$, $c2$ and $c3$, we can write the following generalized version of the function *dot*, which can be used for either adapter:

```
/* This is the function  dot  as it will be used */
dot(X, Y) int X, Y;
{ int offset;
  char ch;
  offset= 0x2000*(Y&c1) + c2*(Y>>c3) + (X>>3);
  peek(0xB800, offset, &ch, 1);
  ch |= 0x80 >> (X&7);
  poke(0xB800, offset, &ch, 1);
}
```

We now have to take care that appropriate values are assigned to $c1$, $c2$, $c3$, and we shall let this occur only at execution time. In this way the programs which use our graphics functions will run on any IBM (compatible) PC, provided it has either a monochrome graphics or a color graphics adapter. An awkward solution would be to let our program ask the user which adapter type applies. Fortunately, this is not necessary. We can instead use the BIOS routine associated with software interrupt 11H, which determines whether or not the color graphics adapter has been installed. If not, the monochrome graphics adapter ought to be present, but we shall not rely on this, since, instead, there might be the monochrome display adapter, which can display characters only. If, after a call of software interrupt 11H, at least one of the bits 4 and 5 is zero, the equipment contains a color graphics adapter. The situation is more difficult if these two bits are set, for then we have to check if there is really a monochrome graphics adapter. We shall perform this check by trying to write something into address 0xB8000 and subsequently reading it. If this attempt fails, that is, if we read something different from what we have written, there is no graphics adapter. If it succeeds, we know that there is one, and since it is not the color graphics adapter, we assume that it is the monochrome graphics adapter. The function *iscolor,* listed below, returns the value:

> 1 if there is a color graphics adapter,
> 0 if there is a monochrome graphics adapter,
> −1 if there is a monochrome display adapter (not suitable for graphics).

```
#include "dos.h"
union REGS regs;

int iscolor()
{ char ch0, ch1, x;
  int86(0x11, &regs, &regs);
  if ((regs.x.ax & 0x30) != 0x30) return 1;   /* Color graphics        */
  outp(0x3BF, 3);                  /* Configuration switch, see Section 2.6 */
  peek(0xB800, 0, &ch0, 1);   /* Try to read ch0 from screen memory    */
  ch1 = ch0 ^ 0xFF;           /* Find some value different from  ch0   */
  poke(0xB800, 0, &ch1, 1);   /* Try to write this into screen memory  */
  peek(0xB800, 0, &x, 1);     /* Try to read the latter value          */
  poke(0xB800, 0, &ch0, 1);   /* Restore the old value   ch0           */
  return ( x == ch1 ? 0 : -1) /* Has written value been read?          */
}
```

Although we can use this function whenever we wish, it would be unwise to call it in the function *dot,* because the latter function is called a great many times and should therefore be as fast as possible. We still have to develop the function *initgr,* to initialize graphics mode, and this is where *iscolor* is needed, as the next section shows.

2.6 ENTERING GRAPHICS MODE

We distinguish two states of the machine, called *text mode* and *graphics mode.* Normally the machine is in text mode, which means that characters are displayed on the screen by a character generator. The ASCII values of these characters, each with a so-called attribute, are stored in the adapter (which need not be a graphics adapter), as we discussed in Section 1.3. Our graphics functions will work only if we switch to graphics mode, also called *bit-mapped* mode. We have to be careful with this, because in graphics mode the operating system cannot display any messages, and if we enter text on the keyboard it is not echoed on the screen. In the Sections 2.8 and 2.9 we shall deal with this in detail. If we wish to enter graphics mode, things are again somewhat easier with a color graphics adapter than with a monochrome graphics adapter. In either case we shall use the function *initgr,* but the adapter-dependent part of its task will be delegated to one of the two functions *initcolgr* and *initmongr,* depending on the adapter type. As discussed in Section 2.5, another task of *initgr* will be to inquire which adapter is used. Once this is known, some important global variables will be given their appropriate values:

```
int in_textmode=1, colorgr, X__max, Y__max;
static int c1, c2, c3;
float x_max=10.0, y_max=7.0, horfact, vertfact;

/* This is an initialization function for graphics */

initgr()
{ if (!in_textmode) error("initgr is called in graphics mode");
  colorgr = iscolor();
  if (colorgr < 0) error("Wrong display adapter");
  if (colorgr)
  { initcolgr(); /* Enter graphics mode (color graphics)    */
    X__max = 639; Y__max = 199;
    c1 = 1; c2 = 80; c3 = 1;
  } else
  { initmongr(); /* Enter graphics mode (monochrome graphics */
    X__max = 719; Y__max = 347;
    c1 = 3; c2 = 90; c3 = 2;
  }
  in_textmode=0;
  horfact = X__max/x_max; vertfact = Y__max/y_max;
}
```

We have also defined the variables $X__max$, $Y__max$, x_max, y_max, *horfact*, *vertfact*, all mentioned in Section 2.1, and the new variables $c1$, $c2$, $c3$, *in_textmode, colorgr*. Recall that the keyword *static* implies that these (external) variables are not published to the linker, so other modules have no access to them and consequently cannot alter them. We omit this keyword for variables which might be useful in the programs where the graphics functions are called. Introducing the variables *in_textmode* and *colorgr* is not strictly necessary, but they may be handy. We shall use *in_textmode* in some functions (such as *initgr*) to check whether those functions are called in the correct mode. For example, if *initgr* is called when the machine is already in graphics mode, we will give an error message and stop program execution. Also, in complicated programs, we can use this external variable ourselves to ask in which mode the machine is. The variable *colorgr* can be used to inquire which adapter is used, without calling the function *iscolor* each time.

We now have to perform the actual task of entering graphics mode. With the color graphics adapter, we can use a BIOS routine for this purpose. We shall use software interrupt 10H twice. There are several video states for this adapter, and the current one can be inquired by placing code 15 into register AH. We shall do this, and store the obtained information into the variable *old_vid_state*. This enables us to restore this video state later when we revert to text mode. For the actual transition to graphics mode, we have to place code 0 into register AH. To obtain the specific video state with resolution 640×200, we also have to place the value 6 into register AL:

```
static int old_vid_state;

/* This function switches to graphics mode (color graphics): */

initcolgr()
{ regs.h.ah = 15; /* Inquire current video state */
  int86(0x10, &regs, &regs);
  old_vid_state = regs.h.al;

  regs.h.ah = 0;   /* Set graphics mode        */
  regs.h.al = 6;   /* 640 x 200, black/white   */
  int86(0x10, &regs, &regs);
}
```

The variable *regs* must have been defined as in Section 2.5. This definition is not repeated here because we shall combine everything into one module, in which that definition occurs only once.

For the monochrome graphics adapter, we cannot use any BIOS routine, so we have to perform very low-level operations ourselves. As we have seen in Section 1.2, we can use the function *outp* to perform elementary output instructions. We shall briefly describe what we shall do, without discussing each step in detail. More information about this can be found in Sargent and Shoemaker (1984) and in the documentation of your monochrome graphics adapter, if you have any. Switching to graphics mode takes five steps:

Step 1. We send the value 3 to output port 3BF, the so-called *Configuration Switch*. To this end we write

```
outp(0x3BF, 3);
```

This call sets the bits 0 and 1 of the switch, with the effect that now both graphics pages (0 and 1) can be used (although we will use only page 1). When these bits are zero, the Configuration Switch protects against accidental setting of graphics mode. This first step is mentioned here for the sake of completeness. Actually we performed this action already when we determined which adapter was used in the function *iscolor*. We have discussed this in Section 2.5.

Step 2. We send the value 0x82 to the output port 3B8, the so-called *Display Mode Control Port*:

```
outp(0x3B8, 0x82);
```

Since the value 0x82 reads 1000 0010 in binary, the bits 7 and 1 are set, and the bits 6, 5, 4, 3, 2, 0 are cleared. Setting bit 1 is the most essential action in the whole operation of switching from text mode to graphics mode. We select page 1, starting at 0xB8000, by setting bit 7, otherwise, page 0, starting at 0xB0000 would be displayed. Another important action in this step is clearing bit 3. This has the effect that the video display is disabled until we set this bit, see Step 5. We thus avoid the screen to be blinking in an irritating way during the actions of the next steps.

Step 3. The registers 0, ... , 11 of the 6845 CRT controller are now to be given the values required for operating in graphics mode. These values are related to the way a raster display works. Since explaining them would involve quite technical hardware aspects, I shall simply list these values in decimal notation:

Register: 0 1 2 3 4 5 6 7 8 9 10 11
Value: 53 45 46 7 91 2 87 87 2 3 0 0

We can give these registers the required values by using only two ports, namely:

03B4, the 6845 Index Register;
03B5, the 6845 Data Register.

We first place the register number (0, ... , 11) into the index register, and then write the required value into the data register. For example, register 0 is given the value 53 as follows:

```
outp(0x3B4, 0);  /* select register 0          */
outp(0x3B5, 53); /* assign the value 53 to it */
```

Step 4. We fill the entire graphics page 1 (32K bytes, starting at address B8000) with binary zeros. We shall use the function *poke,* described in Section 1.2, and copy a sequence of 128 consecutive bytes in each call of this function, which is considerably faster than copying one byte at a time. We define an array, called *zeros* and containing 128 zero bytes, and write:

```
for (j=0; j<256; j++) poke(0xB800, j << 7, zeros, 128);
```

Since $j \ll 7$ is equivalent to $j*128$, the starting addresses are successively 0, 128, 256, . . . , and altogether we copy $256 \times 128 = 32768$ bytes.

Step 5. We send the bit sequence 1000 1010 (hexadecimal 8A) to the Control Port 3B8. Bit 3 is now set, which means that the video display is enabled, see also Step 2.

The function *initmongr* includes comments referring to the above steps:

```
static char
   gtable[12] = {53, 45, 46,  7, 91, 2, 87, 87, 2,  3,  0,  0},
   zeros[128]; /* implicitly initialized to zero */

/* This function switches to graphics mode (monochrome graphics): */

initmongr()
{ int i, j;
  outp(0x3BF, 3);               /* Step 1 */
  outp(0x3B8, 0x82);            /* Step 2 */

  for (i=0; i<12; i++)
  { outp(0x3B4, i);
    outp(0x3B5, gtable[i]);    /* Step 3 */
  }
  for (j=0; j<256; j++) poke(0xB800, j << 7, zeros, 128);
                                /* Step 4 */

  outp(0x3B8, 0x8A);            /* Step 5 */
}
```

2.7 QUITTING GRAPHICS MODE

To quit graphics mode and revert to text mode we shall use the function *endgr,* promised in Section 1.1. However, we have to be careful with this. Reverting to text mode will clear the screen, so if this takes place immediately after our picture has been completed, we will not have enough time to have a look at it! Displaying the picture for a fixed period of time would not be completely satisfactory. A much better solution is to let the picture remain on the screen until we have typed something on the keyboard. If we used *scanf* or *getchar* for this purpose, then reading a single character would not always work, because many programs read numbers at the beginning of program execution and such a number sequence is usually followed by a newline character, entered by pressing the RETURN or ENTER key. That newline character is then still present in the input buffer and will immediately turn up as the next character that is read. To solve this problem, we could read two characters, adopting the convention that one or two characters are to be entered as a signal that complete picture is to disappear from the screen. There is, however, a better solution. Instead of *scanf* or *getchar,* we can use the function *getch,* which reads directly from the keyboard, not from the 'standard input file' *stdin.* Other nice features of *getch* are that it does not echo the character on the display, which in graphics mode is undesirable, and that it reads the character as soon as the key for that character is pressed. (As you will know, *getchar* and *scanf* will actually read the entered characters only when the RETURN key is pressed, enabling us to use the backspace key as long as this has not happened).

Here is the function endgr as we will use it:

```
endgr()
{ getch();
  /* Wait until a key is pressed */
  to_text();
}
```

The actual task of reverting to text mode will be performed by the function *to_text.* Incidentally, defining the function *to_text* for this task enables us to use it ourselves as well, and to revert to text mode immediately if this should be required. Similar to what we did in Section 2.6, we shall define two adapter-dependent functions *endcolgr* and *endmongr,* and call the one that applies:

```
to_text()
{ if (in_textmode) error("endgr or to_text is called in text mode");
  if (colorgr) endcolgr(); else endmongr();
}
```

For the *color* graphics adapter, we write:

```
/* This function reverts to text mode (color graphics): */

endcolgr()
{ regs.h.ah = 0; regs.h.al = old_vid_state;
  int86(0x10, &regs, &regs);
}
```

For the *monochrome* graphics adapter, we again have to perform more elementary actions ourselves:

Step 1. We send the value 0 to the Display Mode Control Port:

```
outp(0x3B8, 0);
```

> Since bit 1 is made zero, this call already returns to text mode. However, also bit 3 is cleared, and this disables the video display, see also Step 2 in Section 2.6, where we discussed the function *initmongr.*

Step 2. As in Step 3 in Section 2.6, we have to place certain values into the registers $0, \ldots, 11$ of the 6845 CRT Controller. Again, we shall not go into technical details, but simply list the required values:

Register: 0 1 2 3 4 5 6 7 8 9 10 11
Value: 97 80 82 15 25 6 25 25 2 13 11 12

Step 3. We place blank spaces into screen memory. For each character, two bytes have to be written:

> a space character, ASCII value hex. 40;
> an attribute value, 7.

We call the function *poke* 256 times, each time copying 16 bytes, which amounts to $256 \times 16 = 4096$ bytes. On the screen we have 25 lines of 80 position, which are 2000 positions. Since for each position we need both a value and an attribute byte, we actually use $2000 \times 2 = 4000$ bytes.

Step 4. We send the bit sequence 0000 1000 (hexadecimal 08) to the Control Port 3B8. By setting bit 3, the video display is enabled, see also Step 1.

The function *endmongr* shows the corresponding program text:

```
static char ttable[12] = {97, 80, 82, 15, 25, 6, 25, 25, 2, 13, 11, 12};

/* This function reverts to text mode (monochrome graphics): */

endmongr()
{ int i, j;
  outp(0x3B8, 0);                                    /* Step 1 */
  for (i=0; i<12; i++)
  { outp(0x3B4, i);                                  /* Step 2 */
    outp(0x3B5, ttable[i]);
  }
  for (j=0; j<256; j++) poke(0xB000, j << 4,         /* Step 3 */
    "\40\7\40\7\40\7\40\7\40\7\40\7\40\7\40\7", 16);
  outp(0x3B8, 0x08);                                 /* Step 4 */
}
```

2.8 ABNORMAL PROGRAM TERMINATION

At the beginning of this Chapter we used the function *check* to test whether a given point (X, Y) lies inside the screen boundaries. In itself this test is trivial, but the problem is what we should do if the test fails. We shall not attempt to repair the error, but try to print an error message and terminate the program by the call *exit*(1). However, when our system is in graphics mode, we first have to revert to text mode. We could decide to revert to text mode immediately, using the function *to_text*, shown in Section 2.7, since in this case the picture will probably be a failure, not worth looking at. On the other hand, we might need the information shown by the portion of the picture produced so far to debug our program. This suggests to let the computer wait until a key is pressed on the keyboard, just like we did in the function *endgr*. However, this has another undesirable aspect, namely that in time-consuming graphics programs such as those for hidden-line elimination (as explained in my previous graphics book), we would simply be waiting for the machine, not knowing that it cannot proceed because of an error, and is in fact waiting for us! The simple solution we shall adopt is to draw a full diagonal from the left-bottom to the right-top corner of the screen, as a signal from the computer that something is wrong and that we have to press any key to revert to text mode, upon which an error message will be displayed. Before we press a key, we have as much time as we wish to observe the graphics results produced so far. We shall use the following function *fatal*. It is called in the function *check* if the position of the given point turns out to be invalid, but we can also call it in our own programs in case of a fatal error, which requires reverting to text mode. Notice that the function does not terminate program execution but returns to its caller. A call of *fatal* is usually followed by printing an error message, after which we call the function *exit*. Here are the two functions:

```
fatal()
{ draw_line(0, Y__max,  X__max, 0); endgr();
}

check(X, Y) int X, Y;
{ if (X < 0 || X > X__max || Y < 0 || Y > Y__max)
  { fatal();
    printf("Point outside screen (X and Y are pixel coordinates):\n");
    printf("X = %d       Y = %d\n", X, Y);
    printf("x = %10.3f   y = %10.3f\n",
    X/horfact, (Y__max-Y)/vertfact);
    exit(1);
  }
}
```

The arguments of this function are pixel coordinates, but the user will think in terms of user's coordinates, so we approximately compute the original coordinates x and y from X and Y. Recall that in graphics mode the operating system cannot print any error messages in case of serious fatal errors, such as stack overflow. The prevention of such error situations is therefore extremely important in graphics programs. With respect to stack overflow, which might occur in recursive programs, it is wise to take care that more memory space is available for the stack than the default size of, say, 2048 bytes. In Lattice C, we can specify the maximum stack size by writing, for example,

```
unsigned int _STACK = 15000;
```

to define a maximum stack size of 15000 bytes. We shall include this line in our graphics package.

2.9   USING THE BREAK KEY IN GRAPHICS MODE

Our graphics functions, developed in the preceding sections, are not yet complete. If they were used in that form, any attempt to use a console break while in graphics mode would have either a very undesirable effect or no effect at all. As we have seen in Section 1.2, the operating system will not always listen to our pressing Ctrl Break or Ctrl C. The function *checkbreak,* listed in Subsection 1.2.4, will remedy this, so we shall call it in some graphics function that is frequently used. Since such a call is rather innocent, it is not very critical where we place it. We shall use the function *draw_line* for this purpose. Later we shall extend our set of graphics functions, and then we shall call *checkbreak* at some other places as well. Instead, we could have used the function *dot,* but as this function is called extremely frequently, we had better avoid any time-consuming check here.

There is a more serious problem, however. Let us assume that, as a result of our calling *checkbreak,* the machine will listen to our console-break attempt. If this occurs when the computer is in graphics mode, then, without special measures, it will 'hang up' the system to such an extent that the machine seems to be out of order. Only after turning it off and on it will work properly again. There is a simple explanation for this. When a program is interrupted by a console break, the default interrupt handler will simply terminate its execution. This does not include returning to text mode, which is essential if the system is in graphics mode. Thus we have to supply our own function, similar to *my_function* in Subsection 1.2.4. We shall call it *brfun,* and define it as follows:

```
int brfun()
{ to_text(); exit();
}
```

At the beginning of the function *initgr* we insert:

```
onbreak(brfun);
```

After this statement, a console break will result in a call of *brfun,* so the system will first revert to text mode and then stop program execution.

Normally, the function *to_text* is not called in *brfun* but elsewhere, such as in the function *endgr.* After such a normal call of *to_text,* our program may not finish immediately but perform some task where again it might be desirable to stop it by means of a console break. Since the system is then in text mode, the default interrupt handler should be activated, not our function *brfun.* So when reverting to text mode, we shall restore the default interrupt handler. To achieve this we only have to insert the statement

```
onbreak(0);
```

in the function *to_text.*

As a result of what we have discussed in this section, the functions *initgr, to_text* and *draw_line* in the module LINDRAW.C (listed in Section 2.10) will slightly differ from their versions discussed in the preceding sections. Besides calling *checkbreak,* we shall perform another new task in *draw_line.* This function ought to be called only in graphics mode, and it is worthwhile to check this. Sometimes we may forget to include a call of *initgr* in our programs, and it is nice to have a decent error message in this case. Recall that the variable *in_textmode* was introduced for this purpose, so we will insert the line

```
if (in_textmode) error("Not in graphics mode (call initgr.)");
```

in *draw_line.*

2.10   A PACKAGE FOR LINE DRAWING

In this section we shall combine the functions of this chapter into one module, which, after compilation can be loaded along with a main program which uses some of these functions:

```
/* LINDRAW.C: A package of routines for line drawing, see also
              PROGRAMMING PRINCIPLES IN COMPUTER GRAPHICS,
              by L. Ammeraal                                   */

#include "dos.h"
union REGS regs;
unsigned int _STACK = 15000;
int in_textmode=1, colorgr, X__max, Y__max;
static int c1, c2, c3, old_vid_state, X1, Y1;
float x_max=10.0, y_max=7.0, horfact, vertfact;
static char
    gtable[12] = {53, 45, 46,  7, 91, 2, 87, 87, 2,  3,  0,  0},
    ttable[12] = {97, 80, 82, 15, 25, 6, 25, 25, 2, 13, 11, 12},
    zeros[128]; /* implicitly initialized to zero */

int IX(x) float x; { return (int)(x*horfact+0.5); }
int IY(y) float y; { return Y__max-(int)(y*vertfact+0.5); }

initgr()  /* Initialize graphics */
{ int brfun();
  if (!in_textmode) error("initgr is called in graphics mode");
  colorgr = iscolor();
  if (colorgr < 0) error("Wrong display adapter");
  onbreak(brfun);                 /* Set break trap */
  if (colorgr)
  { initcolgr(); /* Enter graphics mode (color graphics)    */
    X__max = 639; Y__max = 199;
    c1 = 1; c2 = 80; c3 = 1;
  } else
  { initmongr(); /* Enter graphics mode (monochrome graphics */
    X__max = 719; Y__max = 347;
    c1 = 3; c2 = 90; c3 = 2;
  }
  in_textmode=0;
  horfact = X__max/x_max; vertfact = Y__max/y_max;
}

initcolgr()   /* Switch to graphics mode (color graphics) */
{ regs.h.ah = 15; /* Inquire current video state */
  int86(0x10, &regs, &regs);
  old_vid_state = regs.h.al;

  regs.h.ah = 0;  /* Set graphics mode         */
  regs.h.al = 6;  /* 640 x 200, black/white    */
  int86(0x10, &regs, &regs);
}

initmongr() /* Switch to graphics mode (monochrome graphics) */
{ int i, j;                    /* See Section 2.6   */
/* outp(0x3BF, 3);    Step 1, already dealt with in  iscolor */
  outp(0x3B8, 0x82);                /* Step 2 */

  for (i=0; i<12; i++)
  { outp(0x3B4, i);
    outp(0x3B5, gtable[i]);   /* Step 3 */
  }
  for (j=0; j<256; j++) poke(0xB800, j << 7, zeros, 128);
                                  /* Step 4 */

  outp(0x3B8, 0x8A);              /* Step 5 */
}

endgr()
/* Wait until any key is hit and revert to text mode   */
```

```
{ getch();
  to_text();
}


to_text()
/* Revert to text mode */
{ if (in_textmode) error("endgr or to_text is called in text mode");
  if (colorgr) endcolgr(); else endmongr();
  in_textmode = 1;
  onbreak(0);  /* Restore default break interrupt handler */
}


endcolgr()
/* Revert to text mode (color graphics): */
{ regs.h.ah = 0; regs.h.al = old_vid_state;
  int86(0x10, &regs, &regs);
}


endmongr()
/* Revert to text mode (monochrome graphics): */
{ int i, j;                                          /* See Section 2.7 */
  outp(0x3B8, 0);                                        /* Step 1 */
  for (i=0; i<12; i++)
  { outp(0x3B4, i);                                      /* Step 2 */
    outp(0x3B5, ttable[i]);
  }
  for (j=0; j<256; j++) poke(0xB000, j << 4,             /* Step 3 */
    "\40\7\40\7\40\7\40\7\40\7\40\7\40\7\40\7", 16);
  outp(0x3B8, 0x08);                                     /* Step 4 */
}


error(str) char *str;
/* Display a message and terminate program execution */
{ if (!in_textmode) to_text();
  printf("%s\n", str); exit(1);
}


move(x, y) double x, y;
/* Move the current point to (x, y);
   x and y are screen coordinates */
{ X1 = IX(x); Y1 = IY(y); check(X1, Y1);
}


draw(x, y) double x, y;
/* Draw a line segment from the current point to  (x, y) */
{ int X2, Y2;
  X2 = IX(x); Y2 = IY(y); check(X2, Y2);
  draw_line(X1, Y1, X2, Y2);
  X1 = X2; Y1 = Y2;
}


draw_line(X1, Y1, X2, Y2) int X1, Y1, X2, Y2;
/* Draw the line segment from (X1, Y1) to (X2, Y2);
   X1, Y1, X2, Y2 are pixel coordinates  */
{ int X, Y, T, E, dX, dY, denom, Xinc = 1, Yinc = 1,
  vertlonger = 0, aux;
  checkbreak();              /* To make DOS check for console break */
  if (in_textmode) error("Not in graphics mode (call initgr)");
  dX = X2 - X1; dY = Y2 - Y1;
  if (dX < 0) {Xinc = -1; dX = -dX;}
  if (dY < 0) {Yinc = -1; dY = -dY;}
  if (dY > dX) { vertlonger = 1; aux = dX; dX = dY; dY = aux; }
  denom = dX << 1;
  T = dY << 1;
  E = -dX; X = X1;
  Y = Y1;
```

```
  while (dX-- >= 0)
  { dot(X, Y);
    if ((E += T) > 0)
    { if (vertlonger) X += Xinc; else Y += Yinc;
      E -= denom;
    }
    if (vertlonger) Y += Yinc; else X += Xinc;
  }
}


checkbreak()
{ char ch;
  if (kbhit()) { ch = getch(); kbhit(); ungetch(ch); }
}


dot(X, Y) int X, Y;
/* Light the pixel with coordinates X, Y */
{ int offset;
  char ch;
  offset= 0x2000*(Y&c1) + c2*(Y>>c3) + (X>>3);
  peek(0xB800, offset, &ch, 1);
  ch |= 0x80 >> (X&7);
  poke(0xB800, offset, &ch, 1);
}


int iscolor()    /* Find out which adapter is used */
{ char ch0, ch1, x;
  int86(0x11, &regs, &regs);
  if ((regs.x.ax & 0x30) != 0x30) return 1;    /* Color graphics      */
  outp(0x3BF, 3);                  /* Configuration switch, see Section 2.6 */
  peek(0xB800, 0, &ch0, 1);    /* Try to read ch0 from screen memory    */
  ch1 = ch0 ^ 0xFF;            /* Find some value different from  ch0   */
  poke(0xB800, 0, &ch1, 1);    /* Try to write this into screen memory  */
  peek(0xB800, 0, &x, 1);      /* Try to read the latter value          */
  poke(0xB800, 0, &ch0, 1);    /* Restore the old value   ch0           */
  return ( x == ch1 ? 0 : -1); /* Has written value been read?          */
}


fatal()
/* Draw a diagonal, then wait until a key is pressed, and
     finally revert to text mode                           */
{ draw_line(0, Y__max,  X__max, 0); endgr();
}


check(X, Y) int X, Y;
/* If point (X, Y) lies outside the screen boundaries, then
     call fatal, print the wrong coordinates, and stop.       */
{ if (X < 0 || X > X__max || Y < 0 || Y > Y__max)
  { fatal();
    printf("Point outside screen (X and Y are pixel coordinates):\n");
    printf("X = %d       Y = %d\n", X, Y);
    printf("x = %10.3f    y = %10.3f\n",
    X/horfact, (Y__max-Y)/vertfact);
    exit(1);
  }
}


int brfun()
/* Graphics interrupt handler, dealing with console break  */
{ to_text(); exit(1); /* Before exit, return to text mode! */
}
```

2.11 AN EXAMPLE

In my book *Programming Principles in Computer Graphics,* all programs with
graphics output used only the graphics routines *initgr, move, draw, endgr,* defined
in module LINDRAW.C, so any of these programs would do as an example here.
Yet I will show another sample program, which, besides the four well-known
functions, also uses the external variables *x_max* and *y_max.* Furthermore, the
program may take a lot of time, so it is nice that we can use the break facility if we
wish. We shall begin in the middle of the screen, and draw a square whose diagonals
are horizontal and vertical. As a measure of its size we use half the length of the
diagonals, and this is one inch for this first square. Then four smaller squares will be
drawn, namely in the directions North, South, East and West relative to the original
one. Their size is found by multiplying the size of the original one by a given
'reduction factor'. Similarly, the distance between their centres and that of the
original one is found by multiplying the original size by a given 'distance factor'.
Then the process is invoked recursively in such a way that now the last four squares
act as the original one, and so on. A square is drawn and used to generate new
squares only if its size is greater than a given 'limit', and, at the same time, it lies
inside the screen boundaries.

```
/* MANYSQ.C: This program draws a great many squares */

extern float x_max, y_max;

float size_reduction, distance_factor, limit;

main()
{ printf("Enter 'size reduction', 'distance factor' and 'limit'\n");
  printf("(for example:  0.5      ,          2.5            0.05):\n");
  scanf("%f %f %f", &size_reduction, &distance_factor, &limit);
  initgr();
  move(0.0, 0.0); draw(x_max, 0.0); draw(x_max, y_max);
  draw(0.0, y_max); draw(0.0, 0.0);
  point(0.5 * x_max, 0.5 * y_max, 1.0);
  endgr();
}


point(x, y, size) float x, y, size;
{ float size1, d;
  if (size > limit &&
      x + size < x_max &&
      x - size > 0 &&
      y + size < y_max &&
      y - size > 0)
  { move(x + size, y); draw(x, y + size);
    draw(x - size, y); draw(x, y - size);
    draw(x + size, y);
    size1 = size_reduction * size;
    d = distance_factor * size;
    point(x + d, y, size1);
    point(x, y + d, size1);
    point(x - d, y, size1);
    point(x, y - d, size1);
  }
}
```

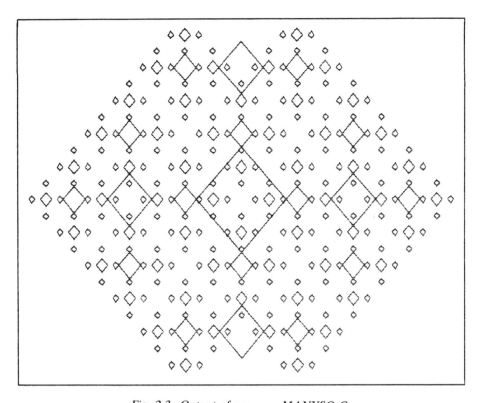

Fig. 2.3. Output of program MANYSQ.C

With the suggested input values 0.5, 2.5, 0.05, the output of this program on the screen is approximately as shown in Fig. 2.3. On the screen, the squares are real squares, but when printed the vertical diagonals are longer than the horizontal ones. We shall cope with this problem in Section 4.4.

CHAPTER 3

Updating the screen

3.1 BIT OPERATIONS APPLIED TO SCREEN MEMORY

So far, all our pictures were static: once something has been drawn, it remains on the screen. If we were restricted to the use of pen plotters, static pictures would be all we could produce. However, with a video display, any pixel that is lit can be made dark again, or, in terms of screen memory, we can reset any bit that was set previously. One way to use this principle is to clear the entire screen and to draw a new picture. This method is particularly suited for *animation* effects. It requires a fast processor, and could best be used in combination with more than one graphics page, as the monochrome graphics adapter has. We can then draw the new picture in the inactive page, and display it only when it has been completed. The very moment an inactive page becomes active, the whole new picture is instantly on screen. If the processor is fast enough, we can realize fast moving pictures, or, in other words, animation in this way. We can fill the entire graphics page with zero bits (which clears the screen) by using the following function:

```
clearpage()
{ int i, n;
  n=(colorgr ? 128 : 256);
    for (i=0; i<n; i++) poke(0xB800, i << 7, zeros, 128);
}
```

Recall that array *zeros* occurred already in the module LINDRAW.C, listed in Section 2.10. It consists of 128 zero bytes, so we write either $128 \times 128 = 16KB$ or $256 \times 128 = 32KB$ with zero bytes into screen memory.

Another approach is to erase just a single portion of the picture, such as a line segment, and to replace it with a new one. An elegant and useful idea in connection with this is to 'toggle', 'invert', or 'flip' the involved bits in the display memory. By this operation these bits are made 0 if they are 1, and 1 if they are 0. As before, let's use X and Y as pixel coordinates, that is,

$$0 \leq X \leq X\_\_max$$
$$0 \leq Y \leq Y\_\_max$$

where $X\_\_max = 719$, $Y\_\_max = 347$ for the monochrome graphics adapter, and $X\_\_max = 639$, $Y\_\_max = 199$ for the color graphics adapter. We now introduce the program variable *drawmode* on which the meaning of the call

```
dot(X, Y)
```

36

depends as follows. The pixel with coordinates X, Y is:

lit   if *drawmode* $= +1$ (write positively),
toggled   if *drawmode* $= 0$ (write alternately),
made dark if *drawmode* $= -1$ (write negatively).

Thus, if *drawmode* $= 1$, the new function *dot* will have the same effect as the one in Chapter 2. If, however, drawmode is 0 or -1, the effect will be different. If it is zero, a dark pixel will be lit and a light pixel will be made dark. Note that in this case several calls *dot*(X, Y) for the same point (X, Y) will cause the state of that point to alternate; for example, if it is initially dark, its state will be light, dark, light, dark, and so on. Finally, if *drawmode* $= -1$, the call *dot*(X, Y) will simply make that pixel dark, regardless of its previous state.

In the C language, changing a certain bit of a byte in each of the above three ways is straightforward and efficient. You should be familiar with the operators

| (bitwise OR)
&   (bitwise AND)
∧   (bitwise EXCLUSIVE OR)

and with the corresponding assignment operators |=, &=, ∧=. (If not, you might consult my previous book *C For Programmers*.) Suppose, for example, that in byte *ch* the kth bit from the left has to be changed ($0 \leq k \leq 7$). Then if *drawmode* has one of the values $+1$, 0, -1, we can write

```
pattern = 0x80 >> k;
if (drawmode == 1) ch |= pattern; else
if (drawmode == -1) ch &= ~pattern; else ch ^= pattern;
```

where *pattern* is a variable of type int. As an example, let us assume
$ch = 1111\ 1001$ (written in binary), $k = 2$, and *drawmode* $= 0$.
Thus, counting from zero and from the left, the second bit of *ch* should be reset (because it is now set!), and all other bits must not alter. By shifting $0x80$ (or, in binary, $0\ldots0\ 1000\ 0000$), k places right, we obtain
$pattern = 0\ldots010\ 0000$
Since $ch \wedge = pattern$ means $ch = ch \wedge pattern$, where $\wedge$ is the exclusive OR operator, we have

Old value of *ch*:	1111 1001
'widened' to type int:	0...0 1111 1001
Value of variable *pattern*:	0...0 0010 0000
Result of exclusive OR operation:	0...0 1101 1001
New value of *ch* (of type char):	1101 1001

So, indeed, the kth bit from the left has been inverted, and the others have not been affected.

In Chapter 2, we discussed a function *dot* using the operator |= in a way similar to what we did here in the case *drawmode* = 1. We now replace it with:

```
int drawmode=1;
static int offset;
static char lastchar;

dot(X, Y) int X, Y;
{ int pattern;
  offset= 0x2000*(Y&c1) + c2*(Y>>c3) + (X>>3);
  peek(0xB800, offset, &lastchar, 1);
  pattern = 0x80 >> (X&7);
  if (drawmode == 1) lastchar |= pattern; else
  if (drawmode == -1) lastchar &= (~pattern); else lastchar ^= pattern;
  poke(0xB800, offset, &lastchar, 1);
}
```

The variables *offset* and *lastchar* have been made (static) external; the reason for this will be clear in Section 3.4.

It is also desirable to add something to the function *draw_line*. Just before the very last brace (}) of that function, we insert the if-statement:

```
if (drawmode == 0) dot(X1, Y1);
```

Very often we draw a figure by a single call of *move*, followed by several calls of *draw*. For example, we draw triangle ABC by the sequence

```
move(xA, yA); draw(xB, yB); draw(xC, yC); draw(xA, yA);
```

As we know, the three calls of *draw* will result in a great many calls of *dot*, each corresponding to a point of the triangle. However, when in 'alternating' mode, it would not be correct if for some point the function *dot* is called precisely twice, for then the second call would delete the point created by the first. But this is what would happen to, for example, point B. It occurs both as the final point of AB and as the initial point of BC. To prevent missing this point in the result, we use a third call of *dot*. Since subsequent calls of *dot* for the same point alternately light and darken that point, the point will be lit after any odd number of calls (provided it is dark initially). The reason of the above conditional call of $dot(X1, Y1)$ will now be clear. (Note that the portion

```
if (drawmode == 0)
```

is not essential, for neither in 'positive' nor in 'negative' drawing mode an extra call $dot(X1, Y1)$ would be harmful. The test was added merely for reasons of efficiency.) The very first point of a succession of connected line segments deserves our special attention. When, in the example of triangle ABC, line segment AB is drawn, an extra call of *dot* for point A seems undesirable, since that point does not belong to a line segment drawn previously. However, it does belong to side CA, so there will be a third call for this point, and the triangle will appear completely. We now see that the result will not be correct if the figure is not closed, that is, if the last point differs from the initial point. The simplest example of such a figure is a single line segment PQ. To draw this correctly in 'alternating' mode, we have to supply an extra call of the initial point ourselves, and write

```
move(xP, yP); dot(xP, yP); draw(xQ, yQ);
```

This is not very nice, but we should not forget that the extra call of *dot* here is required only if

(a) we use alternating mode, and
(b) the involved point is a free endpoint, that is, it does not belong to some other line segment of the figure, and
(c) precision is at stake.

In many applications it will not be noticed if a single pixel on the free end of a line segment is missing, hence (c). In a closed figure (such as a triangle), however, we may miss the pixel of a point that two adjacent line segments have in common, so this is the more important case, which, fortunately, does not require any extra calls of *dot*.

3.2 A ROTATING STAR

It is now time to see the 'alternate' line-drawing mode in action. We shall produce a moving picture which looks like several concentric stars, all of the same size and rotating about their centre. We can draw a star by choosing five points on a circle. If that circle has radius R, and the centre has coordinates $x0$, $y0$, we can, in this order, connect the points

$$(x0 + R \cos \quad 0°, y0 + R \sin \quad 0°)$$
$$(x0 + R \cos 144°, y0 + R \sin 144°)$$
$$(x0 + R \cos 288°, y0 + R \sin 288°)$$
$$(x0 + R \cos \quad 72°, y0 + R \sin \quad 72°)$$
$$(x0 + R \cos 216°, y0 + R \sin 216°)$$
$$(x0 + R \cos \quad 0°, y0 + R \sin \quad 0°)$$

I also used such stars in *Programming Principles in Computer Graphics*, Section 2.7, in an example that demonstrates recursion. Note that the angles above are multiples of 144°, modulo 360°. (For example $72 = 3 \times 144 - 360$.) We shall not use these exact values, however, but multiples of 145° instead of 144°. Furthermore, we shall not stop after drawing one 'misshapen' star, but simply go on, until some key is pressed. Along with drawing new line segments, we shall erase old ones, in the same order as they were drawn. So, except for the beginning, only some fixed number of star-like figures will be on the screen, and they will look like rotating stars. The user will be asked to enter *Nlin*, the number of visible line segments in the moving picture. Then each time, after having drawn a line segment from point

$$(x0 + R \cos (i \, . \, 145°), y0 + R \sin (i \, . \, 145°)),$$

all we have to do is to erase the old line segment drawn from point

$$(x0 + R \cos \{(i - Nlin) \, . \, 145°\}, y0 + R \sin \{(i - Nlin) \, . \, 145°\}),$$

provided i is not less than *Nlin*. Recall that the new drawing mode ('alternate', with *drawmode* $= 0$) enables us to erase line segments in a very simple way, namely in the same way as they are drawn. We shall adapt the module LINDRAW.C as discussed in Section 3.1, and also add some new functions in Section 3.4. Let us call the resulting graphics package GRPACK.C. The following program should be used in connection with this updated module GRPACK.C.

```
/* ROTSTAR.C: Rotating stars */
#include "math.h"
float angle145, x0, y0, R;

main()
{ int i, j, Nlin;
  extern int drawmode;
  extern float x_max, y_max;
  printf("How many line segments in rotating stars? ");
  scanf("%d", &Nlin);
  x0 = 0.5 * x_max; y0 = 0.5 * y_max; R = 0.9 * y0;
  angle145 = 145.0 * atan(1.0)/45.0;
     /* Angle in radians,  145 * pi / 180    */
  drawmode = 0; /* 'Alternating' */
  initgr(); i=0; j = i - Nlin;
  while (!kbhit())
  { if (j >= 0) line(j);
    line(i);
    i++; if (i == 72) i = 0;
    j++; if (j == 72) j = 0;
  }
  endgr();
}

line(k) int k;
{ float alpha, beta;
  alpha = k * angle145; beta = alpha + angle145;
  move(x0 + R * cos(alpha), y0 + R * sin(alpha));
  draw(x0 + R * cos(beta),  y0 + R * sin(beta));
}
```

The function *kbhit*, discussed in Section 1.2, is used in the main program to terminate the while-loop. This function tests whether a key has been hit, and if so, it returns the value 1, which causes the loop to terminate. The character that corresponds to the pressed key is then still available to be read, so the function *endgr* will now not be waiting for a character, but will immediately return to textmode.

The variables i and j denote the numbers of the line segments to be drawn and erased, respectively. For any value $0, 1, \ldots$ of variable i, the call *line*(i) draws line segment i, and when j obtains that value later, the same line segment is erased by the call *line*(j). When i or j obtains the value 72, it is reset to 0. This is allowed, since $72 \times 145 = 10440 = 29 \times 360$, so the difference between the angles computed from $i = 72$ and $i = 0$ is a multiple of $360°$. This measure is desirable for two reasons, related to the imperfections of machine computations in general. First, we wish the program to be capable of running properly for an indefinite period of time, so i and j must not exceed the maximum integer value of the machine. Second, if we compute

$$cos(phi) \quad \text{and} \quad cos(phi + 2 * k * pi)$$

for large integral values of k (where $pi = 3.14159\ldots$) the results, though theoretically equal, may slightly differ, due to the finite precision of our computations. Consequently, without the 'normalization' of i and j to the range $0, \ldots, 71$, our program might try to erase a line segment slightly different from the one that actually was drawn previously, with the effect that some pixels remain lit. (I have actually experienced this effect in a previous version of this program; although it turned out to disappear when I replaced type *float* by *double,* I prefer the normalization in the above version.) It is interesting to execute the program for various values of *Nlin.* For *Nlin* = 1, we see only one line segment at a time, since, in a symbolic notation, it leads to the following sequence of calls:

$line(i = 0)$;
$line(j = 0)$; $line(i = 1)$;
$line(j = 1)$; $line(i = 2)$;
$line(j = 2)$; $line(i = 3)$;

In general we have:

$line(i = 0)$;
$line(i = 1)$;

. . .
. . .
. . .

$line(i = Nlin - 1)$;
$line(j = 0)$; $line(i = Nlin)$;
$line(j = 1)$; $line(i = Nlin + 1)$;

. . .   . . .

so line segment 0 is erased just before line segment *Nlin* is drawn. This explains that for *Nlin* = 5, we see precisely one star at a time, and for *Nlin* = 5n, we see *n* stars at a time, that is, as long as *Nlin* does not exceed the value 75, for at most 15 stars can be visible. For greater values of *Nlin,* the calls *line(i)* will not always draw new line segments, but sometimes also erase old ones. A nice rotating picture is obtained by choosing, for example, *Nlin* = 100. Figure 3.1 gives only an imperfect impression of this picture. First, the loose ends of the broken line are noticed in the printed output more clearly than on the screen, where they are moving, and second, there is a discrepancy between the horizontal and vertical dimensions in the print-out. The latter problem can be solved by a minor program change, as Section 4.4 will show. For still larger values of *Nlin,* such as 300, the figure will alternately grow and shrink, until a number of line segments equal to that value of *Nlin* have been drawn. From that moment on, the number of line segments will be constant. A more detailed analysis of this program is beyond the scope of this book.

We still have to pay some attention to points of intersection. If we use the 'alternating' drawing mode and an even number of lines pass through a point, that point will not be visible in the result. In most cases a point of intersection lies on only two lines, so points of intersection will be more frequently invisible than visible. Figure 3.1 shows examples of both types of points of intersection. The omission of points of intersection is no doubt a disadvantage of the alternating drawing mode, but this disadvantage is amply compensated by the reappearance of points of intersection when all but one of the intersecting lines are erased. Program ROTSTAR.C demonstrates this clearly.

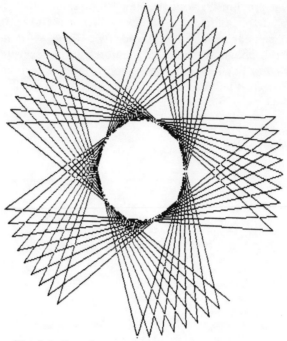

Fig. 3.1. Sample output of program ROTSTAR.C

3.3 A MOVING CURVE

We shall now briefly discuss another program that shows how we can erase line segments. The graphics results may be regarded as modern art; if you do not appreciate this, you and I have the same old-fashioned artistic taste, but I hope you will not mind considering a useless program if this demonstrates some useful programming issues. We shall draw horizontal and vertical line segments of a certain length, the step size, based on a theoretical step size that the user has to specify. (By means of a random number generator, we modify this theoretical stepsize a little to avoid frequent occurrences of partly coinciding line segments.) Similar to what we did in our previous program, we shall add line segments at one endpoint of the 'curve', and erase line segments at the other endpoint. The number of visible line segment, each obtained by a single step, is also to be entered. For each step, a choice is made out of three possibilities:

(1) turning 90° to the left,
(2) turning 90° to the right,
(3) going straight on.

We shall use a random number generator for this choice. However, the user has to specify the relative frequency (expressed as a percentage) that turning either to the left or to the right is to take place. For example, if we enter 80 as the 'percentage of turning steps', then the probabilities of the choices (1), (2), (3), in that order, will be 40, 40, and 20 per cent. For an explanation of the use of random numbers in graphics, I recommend my previous graphics book *Programming Principles in Computer Graphics*. In program MOVCUR.C (see below), we use a linked list to store the coordinates of the visible points, for, in contrast to our previous program, these points can now not be reconstructed by a calculation. At risk of being boring, I recommend my book *C for Programmers* for more information about structures, dynamic memory allocation and linked lists.

```c
/* MOVCUR.C: A moving curve  */
#include "time.h"
int turning;
float step;
extern int drawmode;
main()
{ int i, n, size;
  char ch;
  float xmin=0., xmax=10., ymin=0., ymax=7., x0, y0, x, y;
  struct node { float X, Y; struct node *NEXT; } *front, *rear, *p;
  size=sizeof(struct node);
  printf("Step size (in inches)?"); scanf("%f", &step);
  printf("How many line segments in visible curve?"); scanf("%d", &n);
  n++;
  printf("Percentage of turning steps?"); scanf("%d", &turning);
  printf("Press 1 to start or resume drawing,\n\
       2 to stop,\n\
       3 to terminate program execution.\n");
  do {ch=getch(); if (ch=='2'||ch=='3') exit(0);} while (ch !='1');
  x0=(xmin+xmax)/4; y0=(ymin+ymax)/2;
  front=rear=(struct node *)malloc(size);
  front->X = x0; front->Y = y0;
  initgr(); drawmode=0; i=0;
  while (1)
  { if (kbhit())
    { ch=getch();
      if (ch=='2') { while (!kbhit()); ch=getch(); }
      if (ch=='3') break;
    }
    do
    { gen(x0, y0, &x, &y);
    } while (x<xmin || x>xmax || y<ymin || y>ymax);
    move(x0, y0); draw(x, y);
    if (++i>=n)
    { p=rear; rear= p->NEXT; i=n;
      move(p->X, p->Y); draw(rear->X, rear->Y); free(p);
    }
    p=front; front=(struct node *)malloc(size); p->NEXT = front;
    front->X = x; front->Y = y; x0=x; y0=y;
  }
  endgr();
}

gen(x0, y0, px, py) float x0, y0, *px, *py;
{ int r;
  static int first=1, dir=0;
  long int seed;
  float step1;
  if (first) { first=0; time(&seed); srand((int)seed); }
  r=rand()%100;
  if (r<turning/2) dir=(++dir)%4; else
  if (r<turning)dir=(dir+=3)%4;
  step1=step*(1.+(r-50.)/100.); /* a distortion to avoid accidentally
                                   coinciding lines */
  switch (dir)
  { case 0: *px=x0+step1; *py=y0;       break;
    case 1: *px=x0;       *py=y0+step1; break;
    case 2: *px=x0-step1; *py=y0;       break;
    case 3: *px=x0;       *py=y0-step1; break;
  }
}
```

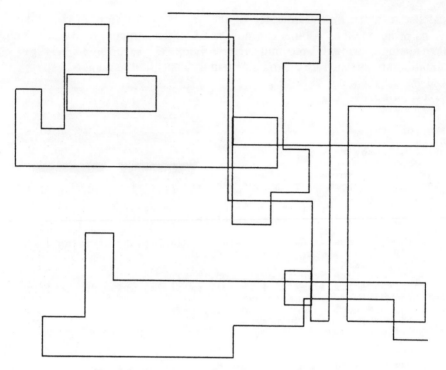

Fig. 3.2. Sample output of program MOVCUR.C

Figure 3.2 shows an example of the output which MOVCUR.C can produce. The input data were:

Step size (inches):   1.0
Number of line segments in visible curve: 100
Percentage of turning steps: 50

Note that the seed for the random number generator is obtained from the function *time*. Since this seed will be different each time the program is executed, the graphics output will also be different each time.

The graphics results of program MOVCUR demonstrates that the if-statement

```
if (drawmode == 0) dot(X1, Y1);
```

added to the function *draw_line* (see Section 3.1) is really useful. It will sometimes happen that two successive line segments have the same direction, and, especially in that case, it is important that the point that joins these two line segments is lit, so that we would not obtain lines with little gaps. Without the above if-statement, this would happen, because then the function *dot* would be called precisely twice for the points in question.

3.4 A FAST ROUTINE FOR AREA FILLING

There is a difference between artists who only draw lines with a pen and those who paint with a brush. So far, we have only drawn lines, but, like painters, we can also

Fig. 3.3. Area filling

fill entire areas. If we have a color graphics adapter and a color monitor, we could produce areas of various colors, but we restrict ourselves to monochrome graphics, so we shall only deal with lighting pixels. We shall do this for all dark pixels inside some closed boundary, consisting of lit pixels. The area thus defined is often a polygon, but it may also contain other polygons, which are then excluded from being filled. Figure 3.3 shows an example of such an area, before and after it is filled. (Dark and light pixels are printed white and black, respectively.)

We want a new function, *fill*, with two floating point arguments, namely the screen coordinates x and y of an inner point of the area to be filled. Starting in this point, it has to look for dark neighboring pixels in all directions, to light them and start from each of them again in all directions, and so on, as long as dark pixels are encountered. So the first thing we need is the following function *pixlit*, which inquires for a given pixel with coordinates X, Y if it is lit.

```
int pixlit(X, Y) int X, Y;
{ int pattern;
  offset= 0x2000*(Y&c1) + c2*(Y>>c3) + (X>>3);
  /* c1, c2 and c3 have been defined in initgr: */
  pattern = 0x80 >> (X&7);
  peek(0xB800, offset, &lastchar, 1);
  return ((lastchar & pattern) != 0);
}
```

This function returns the value of the corresponding bit in screen memory: 1 if the pixel is lit, and 0 if it is dark. Note the similarity between this function and the function *dot*. In *pixlit,* the variable *pattern* is bitwise ANDed to select the bit we need. If that bit is set, the result will be non-zero, otherwise it will be zero. Since we want the returned value to be either 0 or 1, we can simply compare that result with 0, using the inequality operator !=. Whenever speed is at stake, we prefer integer to floating variables, hence the pixel coordinates X and Y. We shall also use a recursive function *pixfill*, which, in contrast to the function *fill*, also has pixel coordinates. For the latter function, we now simply write:

```
fill(x, y) float x, y;
{ pixfill(IX(x), IY(y));
}
```

Recall that the conversion functions *IX* and *IY* were introduced in Section 2.1.
    The remaining problem of writing *pixfill* could theoretically be solved as follows:

```
pixfill(X, Y) int X, Y; /* Not to be used in practice! */
{ if (pixlit(X, Y) == 0)
  { dot(X, Y);
    pixfill(X-1, Y); pixfill(X, Y-1);
    pixfill(X+1, Y); pixfill(X, Y+1);
  }
}
```

From a practical point of view, this version has the following drawbacks:

1. It may need a very large stack;
2. It may take very much time.

    The first point is dangerous, since stack overflow is even worse in graphics mode than in text mode, as we have seen in Section 2.8. Remember that many thousands of pixels may have to be lit, so the recursion depth may grow beyond reasonable proportions. The second point is not nice either. The slowness of this version of *pixfill* is due to the bitwise testing and setting of pixels. We can gain roughly a factor 8 in speed by dealing with entire bytes wherever this is possible. Another awkward aspect is that function *dot* performs a (rather time-consuming) bit selection immediately after function *pixlit* did exactly the same thing. Finally we would save time if we could reduce the recursion depth, and, at least partially, replace recursion with iteration. As shown in Section 3.1, the variables *offset* and *lastchar* are 'static external', which means that they are accessible throughout the module GRPACK.C. (The name GRPACK.C was introduced in Section 3.2.) The functions *pixlit, fill,* and *pixfill* are important enough to be included in this module, so we can use those two static variables in them. In *pixfill,* we shall reduce the recursion depth considerably. All consecutive pixels on horizontal lines will be lit iteratively, and for each line its neighboring lines, if necessary, will be dealt with recursively. Here is the function *pixfill* as we will include it in GRPACK.C; it is explained below:

```
pixfill(X, Y) int X, Y;
  /* Fill a closed region, starting in point (X, Y) */
{ int Xleft, Xright, YY, i, dm;
  char ones=0xFF;
  dm=drawmode; drawmode=1;
  check(X, Y);  /* Defined in GRPACK.C; also used in move and draw */
  checkbreak(); /* See Section 2.9                                 */
  /* Light as many pixels as possible on line Y,
       and determine Xleft and Xright:                 */
  Xleft=Xright=X;
  while (pixlit(Xleft, Y) == 0 && Xleft >= 0)
  { if (lastchar == 0)
    { poke(0xB800, offset, &ones, 1);
      Xleft &= 0xFFF8;
      if (Xright == X) Xright |= 7;
    } else dot(Xleft, Y);
    Xleft--;
  }
  Xright++;
  while (pixlit(Xright, Y) == 0 && Xright <= X__max)
  { if (lastchar == 0)
    { poke(0xB800, offset, &ones, 1);
      Xright |= 7;
    } else dot(Xright, Y);
    Xright++;
  }

  /* Recursive calls of pixfill for at most two remote points: */
  X = (Xleft+Xright) >> 1;
  for (i=-1; i <= 1; i += 2)
  { YY=Y+i;
    while (pixlit(X, YY) == 0) YY += i;
    YY = (Y+YY) >> 1;
    if (pixlit(X, YY) == 0) pixfill(X, YY);
  }

  /* Recursive calls for all dark pixels next to line Y
       (with X values between Xleft and Xright):                 */
  for (YY=Y-1; YY<=Y+1; YY+=2)
  { X=Xleft+1;
    while (X < Xright)
    { i=pixlit(X, YY);
      if (lastchar == ones) X |= 7; else
      if (i == 0) pixfill(X, YY);
      X++;
    }
  }
  drawmode=dm;
}
```

As indicated by comment, this function consists of three parts. In the first while-loop we start in the given point (X, Y), and move to the left, as long as we encounter zero bits. Each time, the variable *Xleft* is the X coordinate of the pixel that is to be dealt with next. However, instead of dealing with one bit at a time, we speed up the process as follows. For each zero bit that is found, we test the variable *lastchar*, to find out if the entire byte to which that bit belongs is zero. If so, we replace that byte with the value 0xFF, and update *Xleft* accordingly. The latter means that *Xleft* is first truncated to a multiple of 8, and then decreased by 1, after which it points to the rightmost bit of the left neighboring byte. After we have found the left endpoint of the line, we look for the right endpoint in a similar way, each time increasing the variable *Xright*. We have to take care that we begin with the correct value of this variable. If the first byte was filled with 0xFF when we were moving to the left, *Xright* should point to the bit immediately to the right of that byte. Otherwise, *Xright* ought to be equal to $X + 1$. When the second while-loop begins in the above function, *Xright* has precisely the correct value in either case. So far the first part of the function, dealing with the horizontal line on which the given point (X, Y) lies. We now have to deal with points above and below this line. My first idea was only to deal with the two neighboring lines recursively. This is implemented in the third part of the function, which we shall consider now, postponing the discussion of the second part. Remember that the pixels to be lit on the two neighboring lines need not form one consecutive sequence, but may consist of several disjunct portions. For each of these lines (with Y-coordinate $YY = Y - 1$, and $YY = Y + 1$), we successively deal with the points (X, YY), where X is now the controlled variable, running from $Xleft + 1$ to $Xright - 1$. We call *pixfill* recursively for all pixels in this range that are dark. Again, we speed up this process by dealing with entire bytes wherever possible. For each bit, we test if the entire byte in which it lies is equal to 0xFF. If so, we increase the running variable X not simply by 1, but such that it points to the bit immediately to the right of that byte. Note that this will occur quite often, since after one recursive call *pitfill*(X, YY), a great number of pixels on line YY will normally be lit. The version of *pixfill* with only parts 1 and 3, can actually be used. The recursion depth of this function is determined by the number of horizontal pixel lines instead of the number of pixels, which makes an enormous difference. However, in complex figures, such as, for example, a spiral, the recursion depth may still exceed the limit imposed by the stack size. If you are not familiar with recursion, the following may be hard to understand, but let me try to explain briefly what is going on. Recursive function calls correspond to the nodes of an (ordered) tree, and the height of this tree is equal to the recursion depth. Usually we want trees to be reasonably balanced in order to restrict their height. In other words, trees should not degenerate into (almost) linear structures. In our function *pixfill*, such a degeneration will occur if, repeatedly, all pixels on one side of line Y are already lit. For that reason, it is wise to insert some additional recursive calls, for points somewhere in the middle of the area to be filled. The second part of function *pixfill* takes care of this. I added it only after experiencing stack overflow, which, as we know, is a nasty error, in particular if it happens in graphics mode. The resulting reduction in recursion depth is enormous. You can verify this yourself, by introducing two global variables *depth* and *maxdepth* to measure the recursion depth as follows:

```
int maxdepth=0, depth=0;

pixfill(X, Y) int X, Y;
{ int Xleft, Xright, YY, i, dm;
  char ones=0xFF;
  if (++depth > maxdepth) maxdepth = depth;
  . . .
  . . .
  . . .
  depth--;
}
```

The value of *maxdepth* should be displayed at the end of program execution (after calling *endgr*); this shows the maximum recursion depth that has occurred during program execution.

We can use the following program AREAFILL.C to experiment with this method of area filling. It draws the screen boundaries and two identical polygons with a hole in them. The program asks for a starting point, and, if this point is not lit, the closed area in which it lies will be filled. In this way, we can choose among various regions to be filled, and for the chosen region we can choose any interior point to start the filling process.

```
/* AREAFILL.C: Area filling and emptying */

main()
{ float x0, y0;
  printf("This program demonstrates area filling.\n");
  printf("x ranges from 0 to 10\n");
  printf("y ranges from 0 to 7\n");
  printf("Enter the coordinates  x, y  of some starting point\n");
  printf("within these ranges:");
  scanf("%f %f", &x0, &y0);
  initgr();
  /* Screen boundary: */
  move(0.0, 0.0); draw(10.0, 0.0); draw(10.0, 7.0);
  draw(0.0, 7.0); draw(0.0, 0.0);
  /* Two copies of the same picture: */
  picture(2.5, 3.5); picture(7.5, 3.5);
  /* Fill the region in which  x0, y0 lies: */
  fill(x0, y0);
  endgr();
}

picture(x, y) float x, y;
{ /* Polygon: */
  move(x+2, y-3); draw(x+2, y-1); draw(x+1.5, y);
  draw(x+2, y+1); draw(x+2, y+3);
  draw(x, y+2); draw(x-2, y+3);
  draw(x-2, y+1); draw(x-1.5, y);
  draw(x-2, y-1); draw(x-2, y-3);
  draw(x-0.5, y-3); draw(x-0.5, y-2.4);
  draw(x-1.5, y-2.4); draw(x-1.5, y-1.8);
  draw(x+1.5, y-1.8); draw(x+1.5, y-2.4);
  draw(x+0.5, y-2.4); draw(x+0.5, y-3); draw(x+2, y-3);
  /* Hole: */
  move(x+0.5, y); draw(x, y+1); draw(x-0.5, y);
  draw(x, y-1); draw(x+0.5, y);
}
```

If we enter the numbers 9.0 and 1.0 as the coordinates x, y of the starting point, the output is Fig. 3.3, shown in the beginning of this section.

3.5 SHADING

Besides filling a closed area with pixels that are lit, as we did in Section 3.4, there are some other possibilities, First, we can use colors if we have a color graphics adapter and a color monitor. Second, with monochrome graphics and only one intensity, we can achieve the effect of several intensities by using a technique called halftoning. This means that, for example, in a square of 3×3 pixels, we distinguish ten different patterns, ranging from all nine pixels dark to all nine pixels lit. This square is then used as a 'superpixel' with ten different intensities $0, 1, \ldots, 9$, corresponding to the number of pixels that are lit. A drawback of this method is the reduced resolution due to the large superpixels. Instead, we can try to use some threshold value for each pixel. Suppose that for each pixel we are given a desired intensity in the form of an integer ranging from 0 to 29. A pixel is dark for the intensity 0 and lit for the intensity 29. For values between 0 and 29 we use the average 14.5 of these extreme values as a threshold. Thus for the values $0, \ldots, 14$ the pixel will be dark, and for the values $15, \ldots, 29$ it will be lit. Unfortunately, this simple method would produce an undesirable effect, called contouring. We obtain a sharp contrast between dark and lit pixels even where darkening should take place only gradually. There is a simple method to avoid this effect. For example, if the intensity of some pixel is 11, it will be dark, so effectively the intensity 0 is used for that pixel. Then we can carry the value 11 to the next pixel. If that pixel was having the intensity 13, we add the carry 11 to it, so that we obtain 24. This lies above the threshold value of 14.5, so that pixel will be lit. As we have now used only the value 24 instead of the theoretical value 29 that belongs to a lit pixel, the carry to the next pixel will be −5, and so on. Here is an example of a horizontal line of desired intensities, with the results of both thresholding methods. Again, the range is $0, \ldots, 29$, so the threshold is 14.5. The letter L denotes a pixel that is lit; a dark pixel appears as a dot (.).

Desired intensities:

    11 13 15 17 19 21 23 23 21 18 14 10 6 5 5 6 8 10 10 10

Results of simple thresholding:

    . . L L L L L L L L . . . .

Results of thresholding with carry:

    . L . L L . L L L . L . . . L . . . L .

In algorithmic terms, the two thresholding methods for the pixels (X, Y), $X = Xmin, \ldots, Xmax$, can be written:

```
/* Simple thresholding: */
for (X = Xmin; X <= Xmax; X++) if (intensity(X, Y) > 14) dot(X, Y);


/* Thresholding with carry: */
carry = 0;
for (X = Xmin; X <= Xmax; X++)
{ carry += intensity(X, Y);
  if (carry > 14)
  { dot(X, Y);
    carry -= 29;
  }
}
```

We shall now discuss a demonstration of thresholding with carry, which has lead to Fig. 3.4.

It is meant as a three-dimensional picture of two spheres. The program that produced this picture will only be clear if we have some idea of how a surface reflects light. Since we have to compute an intensity in a great many pixels, our program would be very time-consuming if we did not make some simplifications. We

Fig. 3.4. Two spheres

shall therefore assume that the direction of the light is the same as the viewing direction, that is, perpendicular to the screen. The main source of light is infinitely far away, so the beams of light are parallel. Besides this source, there will also be an ambient component, which implies that even parts of the object that do not directly receive any light from the source will not be completely dark. Altogether, the intensity of light reflected from a surface consists of three components:

1. An ambient component I_a, due to light scattered back to the object from the surroundings, for example, the walls of a room.
2. A diffuse component I_d, which according to Lambert's cosing law, is proportional to the cosine of the angle θ between the light direction and the normal to the surface.
3. A specular component I_s, which applies in particular to smooth and shiny objects, such as mirrors. For a perfect reflecting surface, the angle of reflection is equal to the angle of incidence.

The way these components are calculated and combined is called the illumination model. Again, our intensities will range from 0 to 29, and, since we don't want our program to be extremely slow, we shall use integer arithmetic wherever possible. Therefore instead of fractions we shall use integer factors k_a, k_d, k_s, which are percentages. The intensity we use will be computed as

$$I = (k_a * I_a + k_d * I_d + k_s * I_s)/100, \qquad (3.1)$$

where all variables have type integer (so I is the truncated quotient). The factors k_a and k_d will be entered by the user. Then k_s is computed as $100 - k_a - k_d$. We use $I_a = 29$, so only I_d and I_s remain to be defined. To produce Fig. 3.4, we begin with the sphere in the background, and we consider the full circle which would represent it in the picture if it were not partly hidden by the sphere in the foreground. We introduce a local coordinate system, the origin O of which coincides with the centre C of that circle. The x- and y-axes lie in the plane of the picture and have the usual directions, so if the circle has a radius r then its equation is

$$x^2 + y^2 = r^2$$

We now imagine a z-axis pointing from C towards us, and for each point (x, y) on or inside the circle we can compute the point (x, y, z) on the sphere, where

$$z = \sqrt{(r^2 - x^2 - y^2)} \tag{3.2}$$

You may wonder if this will lead to a practical method, since there are infinitely many such points. However, the number of pixels inside the circle is finite, and, starting with their pixel coordinates (X, Y), we can compute the corresponding real coordinates x, y, which leads to a finite number of points $P(x, y, z)$ on the sphere. As shown in Fig. 3.5, the normal on the sphere surface in point P has the direction of OP, so the cosine of the angle θ, mentioned above in connection with Lambert's cosine law is

$$\cos \theta = \frac{z}{r} \tag{3.3}$$

Thanks to the chosen direction of the light, we can compute the diffuse component I_d from z and r, without actually calling the cosine function.

We now turn to the specular component I_s, which is associated with the reflected ray shown in Fig. 3.5. If the sphere had a perfect reflecting surface, that ray would

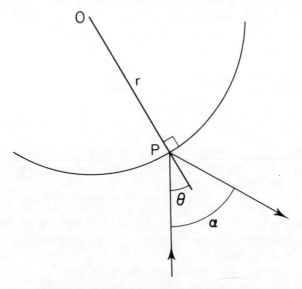

Fig. 3.5. Surface normal and reflected ray

constitute all the light reflected in P as a result of the light reaching P through a ray parallel to the z-axis. In general, a sphere will not be a perfect reflecting surface. The reflected ray of Fig. 3.5 will be the axis of some cone, and the specularly reflected rays of light will lie inside that cone, according to some spatial distribution function. Let α be the angle between the axis of the cone and direction we are interested in, that is, the line of sight. Then we shall use a simple empirical distribution function, due to Bui-Tuong Phong. According to this, the specularly reflected component along the line of sight is proportional to

$$\cos^n \alpha \qquad (|\alpha| \leqq \pi/2)$$

where n is some positive integer. Since the maximum value 1 of this function corresponds to $\alpha = 0$, the intensity in the direction of the cone axis is largest, and the intensity decreases as α increases. The larger the exponent n is chosen, the quicker the intensity decreases with increasing α. If n goes to infinity, the cone degenerates to its axis, so we have to choose n large if the surface is smooth and shiny. In Fig. 3.4 the value $n = 4$ was used (with $k_a = 20$, $k_d = 60$, $k_s = 20$). Recall that in our example both the line of sight and the direction of light that reaches the surface are parallel to the z-axis. As a consequence of this, we have

$$\alpha = 2\theta$$

and

$$\cos \alpha = \cos 2\theta = 2 \cos^2 \theta - 1 = 2 (z/r)^2 - 1$$

Thus we can obtain the values of both $\cos \theta$ and $\cos \alpha$ without using the cosine function. In the innermost loop of our program, all the arithmetic will deal with integers, not with floating variables, let alone functions such as *cos*, *sqrt* and *pow*. It is inevitable that this will reduce the readability of the program, but this price should be paid for otherwise the computation would take ages. The following table shows the meaning of some program variables:

We use integer	instead of floating
ixmax2	$900\,xmax^2$
iz2	$900\,z^2$
ix2[X]	$900\,x^2$
Id2	Id^2
cosa900	$900 \cos \alpha$

We shall also use the functions *setprdim* and *printgr*, which will be discussed in the next chapter. They are used to print the graphics output properly on a matrix printer if this is desired. I included this aspect because otherwise it would not be clear how Fig. 3.4 was produced. On the other hand, the program belongs in this chapter, since it illustrates what we can do with simple monochrome raster graphics. Note in particular that the screen is updated by this program, since the nearer sphere partly overwrites the one in the background, displayed previously. Note also the sharp contrast between this way of producing a perspective picture and the device-independent line-drawing method explained in my book *Programming Principles in Computer Graphics*. Finally, here is the program SHADE.C, which can be used to experiment with various values of k_a, k_d, k_s, and the exponent n of the Phong illumination model. After compilation, this program has to be linked together with GRPACK.OBJ.

```
/* SHADE.C: Two spheres, displayed with shading */
#include "stdio.h"
#include "math.h"
extern float x_max, y_max, horfact, vertfact;
extern int X__max, Y__max, drawmode, colorgr, drawmode;
int c1, c2, c3;

main()
{ int j, k, Xl, Xr, X, Yb, Yt, Y, ka, kd, ks, offset, Ika, n, i,
      I2, sq_root[1000], Id2, Id, Is, I, carry=0, cosa900,
      ix2[720], r2, ixmax2, iz2;
  float x, y, r, fy(), r0, y2, xC, yC, xmax2, xmax,
      xxC[2], yyC[2], rr[2];
  char ch, evenline[90], oddline[90], result[90];
  for (j=0; j<90; j++) { evenline[j]=0x7F; oddline[j]=0xF7; }
  printf("ka, kd and ks are percentages, ka + kd + ks = 100\n");
  printf("(a = ambient, d = diffuse, s = specular)\n");
  printf("\nEnter ka: "); scanf("%d", &ka); Ika = ka * 29;
  printf("\nEnter kd: "); scanf("%d", &kd); ks = 100 - ka - kd;
  printf("\nEnter the exponent n (n = 1, 2, ...) of Phong shading:");
  scanf("%d", &n);
  printf("\nPrinted output required and printer switched on? (Y/N): ");
  do { ch = getchar(); ch = toupper(ch); } while (ch != 'Y' && ch != 'N');
  if (ch == 'Y') setprdim();
  xxC[0] = 0.38 * x_max; xxC[1] = 0.68 * x_max;
  yyC[0] = 0.42 * y_max; yyC[1] = 0.60 * y_max;
  rr[0] = 0.35 * y_max; rr[1] = 0.28 * y_max;
  initgr();
  if (colorgr)
  { c1=1; c2=80; c3=1;
  } else
  { c1=3; c2=90; c3=2;
  }

  /* The intensity ranges from 0 to 29. The background intensity
     is now set.                                                  */

  for (Y=0; Y<=Y__max; Y++)
  { offset = startaddress(Y); /* Address of pixel (0, Y) */
    poke(0xB800, offset, (Y & 1 ? oddline : evenline), c2);
  }

  drawmode = 1;
  for (I2=0; I2<1000; I2++) sq_root[I2] = (int) (sqrt((double) I2) + 0.5);

  for (k=1; k>=0; k--)   /* k is sphere number (0 = nearer sphere) */
  { r0 = rr[k];                        /* Floating             */
    r2 = (int) (r0 * r0 + 0.5);   /* Integer;                   */
    r = sqrt((double) r2);
    xC = xxC[k]; yC = yyC[k];
    for (X=IX(xC-r)-1; X <= IX(xC+r)+1; X++)
    { x = X / horfact - xC;
      ix2[X] = (int) (900.0 * x * x + 0.5);
    }
```

```
Yt = IY(yC + r); Yb = IY(yC - r);      /* Yt < Yb */
for (Y=Yt; Y<=Yb; Y++)
{ y = fy(Y) - yC; y2 = y * y;
  xmax2 = r2 - y2;
  if (xmax2 < 0.0) xmax2 = 0.0;
  ixmax2 = (int) (900.0 * xmax2 + 0.5);
  xmax = sqrt(xmax2);
  X1 = IX(xC - xmax); Xr = IX(xC + xmax);
  for (X=X1; X<=Xr; X++)         /* This loop uses only integers    */
  { iz2 = ixmax2 - ix2[X];       /* iz2 = 900 * z * z               */
        Id2 = iz2/r2;                  /* Square of diffuse intensity     */
        if (Id2 < 0) Id2 = 0;
        Id = sq_root[Id2];            /* Diffuse intensity = 30 cos theta */
        if (Id2 <= 450) Is = 0; else
        { cosa900 = 2 * Id2 - 900;  /* cosa900 = 900 cos alpha         */
          Is = cosa900 / 30;
          for (i=2; i<=n; i++) Is = Is * cosa900 / 900;
                                  /* Exponentiation according to Phong */
        }
        I = (Ika + kd * Id + ks * Is)/100;
        carry += I;
        if (carry > 14)
        { dot(X, Y); carry -= 29;
        } else
        { drawmode = -1; dot(X, Y); drawmode = 1;
        }
      }
    }
  }
  if (ch == 'Y'&& getch())
  { /* Reverse video: */
    for (Y=0; Y <= Y__max; Y++)
    { offset = startaddress(Y);
      peek(0xB800, offset, result, c2);
      for (j=0; j<c2; j++) result[j] ^= 0xFF;
      poke(0xB800, offset, result, c2);
    }
    printgr(0, X__max, 0, Y__max);
  }
  endgr();
}

float fy(Y) int Y; { return (Y__max-Y)/vertfact; }

int startaddress(Y) int Y; /* Start address of pixel (0, Y) */
{ return 0x2000*(Y&c1) + c2*(Y>>c3);
}
```

A note on the module GRPACK.C

In this chapter, we added some functions to the module LINDRAW.C, listed at the end of Chapter 2, and we altered some existing functions. The modified version is called GRPACK.C, and it might disappoint you that this is not listed here. However, some more modifications will follow in Chapter 4, and you can find what you are looking for at the end of that chapter. You can already use GRPACK.C listed there, ignoring some new functions that still have to be dealt with.

CHAPTER 4

Graphics and matrix printers

4.1 PRINCIPLES OF MATRIX PRINTERS

There are two types of popular printers for the PC, namely letter-wheel printers and matrix printers. For text, either printer type has certain advantages over the other. If we want to print text with the quality of a typewriter, a letter-wheel printer is probably the best choice. Matrix printers give less contrast between the black letters and the white background, but they offer considerably more possibilities if in one document we wish to use several letter types and fonts. However, we are now interested not in text but in graphics output, and for this we cannot use a letter-wheel printer, so using matrix printers will be the subject of this chapter. Since matrix printers are less expensive than pen plotters and reasonably suitable for both text and graphics, they are very popular. A nice aspect is the similaity of matrix printers that are produced by various manufacturers. Although there are some minor differences, the common characteristics of most matrix printers are sufficient to achieve all we want. We will try not to use any features and commands which with some printers might cause problems.

Before we can write any software for matrix printers, we need some elementary knowledge of their 'dot graphics' capabilities. If we use a typewriter, we type lines, each consisting of, say, at most 80 characters. In much the same way, a matrix printer, when in graphics mode, prints lines of 'characters', but now each 'character' is a dot pattern, consisting of eight dot positions above one another. Since such a pattern occupies only one dot in the horizontal direction, a great many of them, say, 960, can be placed on the same line. We regard each pattern as a (vertical) column of eight bits, each being 1 if in the position of that bit the dot is present, and 0 if it is absent. We number their positions $0, 1, \ldots, 7$, from bottom to top, so the most significant bit is on the top, instead of on the left as in normal binary notation. As usual, these position numbers are used as exponents of powers of 2, and in this way we assign numbers to the columns. Figure 4.1 shows an example of a pattern, along with the corresponding (magnified) dot column:

```
Bit  pattern        Dot column

        0
        0
        0
        1                  *
        0
        0
        1                  *
        1                  *
```

Fig. 4.1. Bit pattern and dot column

56

Its value is $16 + 2 + 1 = 19$, which in C can be written 0x13. For each pattern to be printed, we have to send its value to the printer in eight bits, that is, in one byte. A sequence of such bytes must be preceded by a printer command that says how many bytes will follow. We shall use a command of the form

ESC 'L' $n1$ $n2$

where

ESC   is the ASCII 'escape symbol', with value 27,
'L'   is character 'L' (with value 76),
$n1, n2$ are two eight bit integers, such that if N is the number of bytes that
           follow, then in C we find $n1$ and $n2$ as follows:

$$n1 = N \% 256;$$
$$n2 = N / 256;$$

Thus we have $N = 256\,n2 + n1$.

4.2 PROGRAMS THAT PRINT GRAPHICS RESULTS

In a C program there are three ways to send data to the matrix printer, or, in more technical terms, to the parallel printer port:

(1) using *fopen* with the symbolic device name LPT1;
(2) directly using the BIOS routine associated with software interrupt 0x17;
(3) directly accessing the I/O ports 0x3BC, 0x3BD, 0x3BE.

These are in fact three levels. In our first program we shall use (1), the highest level. After this, we shall discuss why in practice we prefer (2), the intermediate level. (There is also a note about this choice at the end of this section.) The lowest level, (3), is only mentioned for the sake of completeness; it is used by the software of levels (1) and (2), but we need not bother about this.

Program MATPR1.C shows how we can print a line consisting of 300 copies of the dot pattern shown in Fig. 4.1.

```
/* MATPR1.C: This program prints a line of 300 dot patterns */
#include "stdio.h"
#define N 300

main()
{ int n1, n2, j;
  FILE *fp;
  fp = fopen("lpt1", "wb");              /* Write Binary to printer */
  n1 = N % 256;                          /* n1 = 44                 */
  n2 = N / 256;                          /* n2 = 1                  */
  fprintf(fp, "%c%c%c%c", 27, 'L', n1, n2);
  for (j=0; j<N; j++) putc(19, fp);      /*       300 bit patterns  */
  fclose(fp);
}
```

The output of this program is shown in Fig. 4.2. It consists of 300 columns of which one is shown in Fig. 4.1.

Fig. 4.2. Output of program MATPR1.C

Some points of this program need to be explained. In the call of *fopen*, the name *lpt1* is a reserved file name, which identifies the printer. As the second argument of *fopen* we use the string *"wb"*, which in Lattice C means 'write binary'. The *b* in this string reflects the fact that the bit patterns are to be used literally as binary values, and do not represent normal (printable or non-printable) ASCII characters. The call of *fopen* returns file pointer *fp*, which will now be used whenever something has to be sent to the printer. The first call of *fprintf* sends four bytes to the printer. Their values are

27   76   44   1

Writing

ESC   'L'   44   1

is more readable for us, of course, but the former sequence shows more clearly what is actually sent to the printer. Remember that the format specification %*c* causes the corresponding data item to be written as a character of eight bits, even if that data item is of type int (which occupies 16 bits). In the command

ESC   'L'   *n1*   *n2*

the letter 'L' selects 'double density', which means that horizontally we have 120 dots in an inch. Instead of 'L', we could have used 'K' for 'single density' with 60 dots per inch, and, depending on the printer, there may be some more possible densities. Since in our example we have

$N = 256 . n2 + n1 = 300,$

the printer expects exactly 300 byes to follow this command. After these 300 byes the printer is no longer in graphics mode. In the loop we use the statement

```
putc(19, fp);
```

which has the same effect as

```
printf(fp, "%c", 19);
```

would have had.

I had been using the above method, that is, level (1), for quite a long time without being aware of a trouble spot in it. To my astonishment, however, some day one picture stubbornly refused to be printed, namely Fig. 3.1. Its beginning was printed correctly, but somewhere near the middle the printer stopped. It took me more than a full day of hard testing to find out that bit pattern 0001 1010, that is, 26, caused the trouble. I then looked in a table of ASCII codes, and found that 26 is the code for Ctrl Z, which means 'end of input'. It appeared that the printer, even when in graphics mode, received only 255 out of the 256 possible values of eight bits. As soon as we try to send the value 26, the operating system interprets it as the end of the data stream, so no further data are sent to the printer. Books and manuals are rather silent on this point, so I had to find a remedy myself. I first considered the possibility of simply altering some bit whenever 0001 1010 occurred. This would probably not have been noticed in the results, but yet it would have been incorrect, so I looked for a better solution. Since it is the high-level I/O facilities that perform the undesired test with the character to be printed, we can bypass this test by switching to the lower level of calling a BIOS routine, using a software interrupt. We can send a one-byte value to the parallel printer port, in other words, to the matrix printer, by placing it into register AL, clearing the registers AH and DX, and invoking software interrupt $0x17$.

```
prchar(ch) char ch;     /* Print character          */
{ regs.x.dx=0;          /* Printer selection        */
  regs.h.ah=0;          /* Send byte from AL to printer */
  regs.h.al=ch;         /* Byte to be sent to printer   */
  int86(0x17, &regs, &regs);
}
```

If we wished to insert this source text in our own program, we would also have to insert the two lines

```
#include "dos.h"
union REGS regs;
```

However, we shall add this function to the module GRPACK.C, which already contains these two lines. Strictly speaking, function *prchar* is not merely a function for graphics. It can also be used to send normal characters directly to the printer. However, that can also be done using *fprintf*, as in MATPR1.C, since among normal characters the code 26 will not occur. So it is only in connection with graphics that we really need *prchar*, and from that point of view it is reasonable to extend GRPACK.C with this function. If we link the following program MATPR2.C with this extended module and run it, the printed output will be the same as that of MATPR1.C

```
/* MATPR2.C: This program prints a line of 300 dot patterns */
#include "dos.h"
#define N 300

main()
{ int n1, n2, j;
  n1 = N % 256;                             /* n1 = 44            */
  n2 = N / 256;                             /* n2 = 1             */
  prchar(27); prchar('L'); prchar(n1); prchar(n2);
  for (j=0; j<N; j++) prchar(19);           /*       300 bit patterns */
}
```

If in program MATPR1.C we alter the value 19 into 26, this value is interpreted as Ctrl Z, and the program does not work. Program MATPR2.C, however, works perfectly after such a modification, so these two programs are not equivalent and we prefer the latter program. (See also the note at the end of this section.)

So far, we have printed only one line, even without moving to the beginning of the next line. In general, the printer is in 'graphics mode' only from ESC 'L' $n1$ $n2$ (or some similar command) to the last of the $256.n2 + n1$ bytes that follow. After this, we can print normal characters, and, in particular, we can send a newline character to the printer. In MATPR1.C this would read

   putc('\n', fp)   or   *fprintf(fp, "\n")*

Since we prefer MATPR2.C, we shall use

   prchar('\n')

For '\n' the value 10 (hex. 0x0A) is actually used, so we could write *prchar*(10) or *prchar*(0x0A) instead, but '\n' expresses more clearly what we mean. More importantly, we have to take care that the paper moves upward precisely the distance we want. Without special measures, the paper will probably move upward 1/6 inch, since that is the line spacing used in ordinary printing. In the vertical direction, the distance between two successive dots is 1/72 inch, so if we print columns of 8 dots, we need a line spacing of 8/72 inch to let two successive lines be adjacent. Although this can be done, it is safer to avoid this line spacing; we shall later discuss why. Instead, we shall use only 7-dot columns, so all values will be less than 128, and the line spacing we need will therefore by 7/72 inch. As an example, we shall print six lines of 400 bit patterns each. The only bit patterns used in this example are 0x55 and 0x2A. The corresponding vertical patterns are shown in Fig. 4.3.

```
0x55                    0x2A

      X                        .
      .                        X
      X                        .
      .                        X
      X                        .
      .                        X
      X                        .       Fig. 4.3. Two dot patterns and their values
```

Let us use the numbers 0, 1, 2, 3, 4, 5, for the six lines to be printed. On the lines 0, 2, 4, we shall print the values 0x55 and 0x2A, in that order, in alternating groups of four equal values each. To obtain a nice pattern as a result of the six adjacent lines, the lines 1, 3, 5 will have similar contents, but first four times 0x2A, then four times 0x55, then again four times 0x2A, and so on. Program MATPR3.C is shown below, along with its output in Fig. 4.4.

Fig. 4.4. Output of program MATPR3.C

```
/* MATPR3.C: Six adjacent lines  */

#define N 400
main()
{ int n1, n2, i, j, oddline, oddquadruple;
  prchar(27); prchar('l');  /* ESC 'l': Set line spacing to 7/72 inch */
  prchar('\n'); n1 = N % 256; n2 = N / 256;
  for (i=0; i<6; i++)
  { oddline = i%2;
    prchar(27); prchar('L'); prchar(n1); prchar(n2);
    for (j=0; j<400; j++)
    { oddquadruple = j%8 > 3 ;
      prchar(oddline == oddquadruple ? 0x55 : 0x2A);
    }
    prchar('\n');
  }
  prchar(27); prchar('@');  /* ESC '@': Reset printer to power-up state */
}
```

As for the first two calls of *prchar,* the command

ESC '1'

says that subsequent line-feed commands are to be carried out with 7/72 inch line spacing. There is such a line-feed command on the next line, namely *prchar*('\n'). The variable *oddline* will have the value 1 for lines 1, 3, 5 and 0 for lines 0, 2, 6. The 400 columns of each line are logically divided into 100 quadruples, numbered $0, 1, \ldots, 99$, each consisting of four consecutive columns. The variable *oddquadruple* is 1 for the quadruple $1, 3, \ldots, 99$, and 0 for the quadruples $0, 2, \ldots, 98$. For the very first quadruple, we have

$$oddline = oddquadruple = 0$$

and here the value 0x55 gives the desired bit pattern. If only one of the two variables is 1 (the other still being 0) we need the pattern 0x2A, and if both variables are 1, we need 0x55 again. This explains the conditional expression occurring as an argument of *prchar* in the innermost loop. The command

ESC '@',

given nearly at the end of the program, resets the printer to the power-up state with respect to line spacing.

It still remains to be explained why we should use 7-bit instead of 8-bit columns. Curiously enough, using 8-bit columns could cause two problems which do not occur with 7-bit columns. First, some printers have a DIP switch which, if in the wrong state, causes the 8th bit to be ignored. For ordinary text printing, only seven bits are needed, and when I for the first time tried to product graphics on a matrix printer, I used someone else's printer, which previously had been printing nothing else but text. It took me several hours to find out why a number of thin horizontal white lines occurred in the graphics output. It then appeared that some DIP switch of the printer was on, which meant that the 8th bit of each pattern was ignored, that is, assumed to be 0. After switching it off, the printer used all eight bits and I obtained the correct output. If this were the only problem, we could still use 8-bit columns, which, after all, is somewhat faster than using 7-bit columns. A warning to notice the DIP switches in case of any problems would then have been sufficient. Yet, our 7-bit solution is nice in that it avoids such difficulties: either state of the DIP switch in question will do! However, there is a second argument in favour of 7-bit patterns. The command

ESC '1'

for 7/72 line spacing does not have an equally simple command for 8/72 line spacing, which is required with 8-bit columns. There is a command for that, namely

ESC 'A' 8

but when I tried to use this, I encountered a difference in the way this must be done for two printers. On the STAR NL10 printer, this command becomes effective only after a second command, namely

ESC '2'

but, unfortunately, this extra command must be absent if we use the EPSON LX-80 printer, because here it would set the line spacing to 1/6 inch! I then tried the command

ESC '3' 24

which should set the line spacing to 24/126 (=8/72) inch, but again I encountered discrepancies between various printers. Fortunately, the simple command

ESC '1'

works properly on all printers I have been using, and, especially after considering the first little problem, mentioned above, I decided to avoid these two annoying difficulties, and to use 7-bit graphics. The price we have to pay for this choice is a decrease in performance by a factor 7/8, which is not a dramatic figure compared with what we gain in portability and user-friendliness.

Note

The problem with Ctrl Z mentioned in this section occurred when I was using Lattice C, version 3.0 When I received version 3.1, along with a new manual, I read that this problem had been due to an error and that it had been corrected in the new version. This means that with the new compiler the higher-level method with

```
fopen("lpt1", "wb")
```

works properly for all byte values, including 26. Thus it is no longer necessary to use the somewhat lower level based on software interrupt 17H. Still, I keep using the latter method. It seems to me that, for other users, software interrupt 17H will be less likely to cause any troubles than the compiler-dependent convention of excluding the name *lpt*1 from being used as a normal file name, reserving it for the printer. You may argue that the function *int*86 for software interrupts that we are using now is also compiler dependent, but do not forget that we need software interrupts anyhow (see Section 1.2 and Chapter 2), so we have already assumed that *int*86 (or something equivalent) is available. Another aspect in favour of my choice is that in this way we do not need any standard I/O functions for printing. Consequently, executable graphics programs may now be shorter than they would have been if we had used functions such as *fopen* merely for the sake of printing.

4.3 PRINTING A SCREEN DUMP

After these preliminaries, we now wish to produce a hard copy of our graphics results as these are displayed on the screen. We shall develop the function *printgr,* which fetches information from the screen memory and sends it to the printer.

For the time being, we shall not worry too much about the concrete dimensions in the horizontal and the vertical directions. Without special measures, a circle on the screen will appear as an ellipse on the paper of the printer, but for the moment we will accept that. We shall present a solution for this problem in Section 4.4.

Recall that we use integer pixel coordinates X and Y, where

$$0 \leq X \leq X\_max$$
$$0 \leq Y \leq Y\_max,$$

and point (X_max, Y_max) is the bottom-right corner of the screen. The concrete values of the coordinates of this point are:

$X\_max = 639$ (color graphics) or 719 (monochrome graphics)
$Y\_max = 199$ (color graphics) or 347 (monochrome graphics)

We shall add four arguments to function *printgr*, which denote the boundaries of a rectangular window on the screen. The contents of this window will be printed. The first two arguments are the minimum and the maximum values for X, and the last two arguments are such values for Y. So if the entire screen is to be printed, we shall write

```
printgr(0, X__max, 0, Y__max);
```

Using what we have discussed in the previous sections, we can now write the function *printgr* as follows:

```
printgr(Xlo, Xhi, Ylo, Yhi) int Xlo, Xhi, Ylo, Yhi;
/* Print contents of rectangle on matrix printer */
{ int n1, n2, ncols, i, X, Y, val;
  prchar(27); prchar('1'); /* Line spacing 7/72 inch */
  ncols=Xhi-Xlo+1;
  n1=ncols%256; n2=ncols/256;
  for (i=Ylo; i<=Yhi; i+=7)
  { checkbreak();      /* To make DOS check for console break */
    prchar(27); prchar('L'); prchar(n1); prchar(n2);
    for (X=Xlo; X<=Xhi; X++)
    { val=0;
      for (Y=i; Y<i+7; Y++)
      { val <<= 1; val |= (Y>Yhi ? 0 : pixlit(X, Y));
      }
      prchar(val);
    }
    prchar('\n');
  }
  prchar(27); prchar('@');
}
```

If the color graphics adapter is being used, we should call *printgr* only in graphics mode, since the software interrupt used to revert to text mode clears the graphics page. As discussed in Section 2.7, we normally use the function *endgr* to switch from graphics mode to text mode. This function calls *to_text*, which in turn calls *endcolgr* if the color graphics adapter is being used. In the latter function we use software interrupt 10H for the actual mode switching, and this causes the unfortunate clearing of the graphics page. If you are familiar with assembly language, you can figure this out by studying the system BIOS listing in the IBM PC Technical Reference manual. Due to this clearing the graphics page, we cannot use a program similar to PRGR.C, described below, for a machine with a color graphics adapter.

In our function *endmongr* (see Section 2.7) for the monochrome graphics adapter, we clear the text page, starting at B0000, but we leave graphics page 1, starting at B8000, unaffected. As a result of this, we can use the function *printgr* even when we are back in text mode. Then the graphics results are no longer displayed on the screen, but they are still in the graphics adapter. Using *printgr* in text mode might seem not particular useful, but it really is, since in text mode we can more easily communicate with the computer than in graphics mode. In particular, we can let our program finish (obviously in text mode), and start a new program to print the graphics output produced by its predecessor and still present in screen memory. Since the graphics program itself no longer exists in memory, we may use the term *post mortem* graphics screen dump for this. Using a monochrome graphics adapter myself, I used this method for various illustrations in this book (e.g. Fig. 2.3). There is a tricky point in this, which must not escape our attention. As we are using *printgr*, the function *pixlit* is used to determine the state of the pixels, and the latter function uses the 'constants' c_1, c_2, c_3 for the address calculation involved. However, in Section 2.6 we saw that the values of c_1, c_2, c_3 are determined in the function *initgr*, and in our post-mortem print program we do not wish to enter graphics mode, so *initgr* will not be used. We shall therefore separate the task of determining the graphics constants, and define them in the following function:

```
setgrcon(colorgr) int colorgr;   /* Set graphics constants */
{ if (colorgr)
   { X__max = 639; Y__max = 199;
     c1 = 1; c2 = 80; c3 = 1;
   } else
   { X__max = 719; Y__max = 347;
     c1 = 3; c2 = 90; c3 = 2;
   }
}
```

We shall add this function to GRPACK.C and call it in *initgr*. We can now also use it in our own programs. This happens in the following program, designed to produce a post-mortem graphics screen dump on systems with a monochrome graphics adapter:

```
/* PRGR.C: This program prints the screen on a matrix printer;   */
/*         It can be used with the monochrome graphics adapter,  */
/*         not with the color graphics adapter.                  */

main()
{ extern int X__max, Y__max;
  if (iscolor())                         /* 0: monochrome graphics   */
  { printf("This program is suitable only for monochrome graphics\n");
    exit(1);
  }
  setgrcon(0);
  printgr(0, X__max, 0, Y__max);
}
```

4.4 PRINTING A CIRCLE AS A CIRCLE

There is still one problem to be solved, namely how to get things printed with vertical dimensions that are correct in comparison with those measured horizontally. Expressed more briefly, we want our printer to print a circle as a circle, not as an ellipse. This seems a complex problem, since the density, that is, the number of dots per inch, is different in the two directions, and for the printer these densities are different from those for the video display. As if this were not bad enough, we also have to distinguish between the monochrome and the color graphics adapter, so you might expect that the required analysis and the corresponding program text will be

long and tedious. Fortunately, that will not be the case. We will retain the principle
of a one-to-one mapping from pixels of the screen to dots on the paper. This means
that both on the screen and on paper (and for both adapter types!) we use
non-negative integer corrdinates X and Y with $X\_\_max$ and $Y\_\_max$ as their
maximum values. Besides these integer coordinates, we have introduced real
coordinates x and y, which have the nice property that unit lengths of both
coordinates have about the same length on the screen: if both x and y are increased
by one, we move about one inch to the right and about the same distance upward.
We achieved this by defining

$$x\_max = 10.0; \qquad y\_max = 7.0;$$

in Section 2.1. The values 10.0 and 7.0 were based on the dimensions of the screen.
They are nice round numbers, so I preferred them to the actual dimensions I
measured, namely 8.27×5.58 inch. It is their ratio that matters, and we have:

$$10.0/7.0 = 1.43 \quad \text{and} \quad 8.27/5.58 = 1.48$$

If instead of 10.0 and 7.0 the more accurate values 8.27 and 5.58 had been chosen
for x_max and y_max, one inch measured horizontally or vertically on the screen
would have corresponded to a difference in our real x and y coordinates of 1, and, in
particular, drawing a circle on the screen would have given a slightly better result
than it does now. These considerations lead us to the solution of our problem. Now
that we are using the printer, x_max and y_max should be based on maximum
dimensions measured on paper, not on the screen, and, since on paper it is nice to
have exact dimensions, we won't sacrifice accuracy to obtain round numbers this
time. The largest rectangle we can draw, expressed in pixel coordinates as

$$0 \leqq X \leqq X\_\_max$$
$$0 \leqq Y \leqq Y\_\_max$$

will have a length of x_max and a width of y_max inches, provided that x_max and
y_max have been defined correctly. This means that all we have to do is to redefine
x_max and y_max as the dimensions of that largest rectangle as it will appear on
paper. Since on paper the horizontal density is 120 dots per inch, the longest
horizontal line, consisting of $X\_\_max + 1$ dots both on the screen and on paper, will
occupy exactly $(X\_\_max + 1)/120$ inches when it is printed. This is the value we
have to assign to x_max. Similarly, since the vertical density is 72 dots per inch, the
value $(Y\_\_max + 1)/72$ is to be assigned to y_max. Here is a function which
performs such a redefinition:

```
/* This function sets x_max and y_max such that graphics
   results will eventually be printed with correct
   dimensions, both horizontally and vertically */
setprdim()
{ extern float x_max, y_max;
  extern int X__max, Y__max;
  setgrcon(iscolor());
  x_max = (X__max + 1)/120.0; y_max=(Y__max + 1)/72.0;
}
```

Note that, before using $X\_\_max$ and $Y\_\_max$, these variables must be defined
depending on the graphics adapter that is used. The function *setgrcon* is therefore
called in this function to give these variables their proper values. When, after calling

setprdim, we call *initgr,* the new values of *x_max* and *y_max* will be used to compute the values of *horfact* and *vertfact,* which from then on are used by the function *IX* and *IY* to derive all pixel coordinates *X* and *Y* from the corresponding real coordinates *x* and *y.* As users, we need not worry about all this. The only important thing is that function *setprdim* can best be called as soon as possible, in any case before *initgr* is called, and also before any use of *x_max* and *y_max* is made. We shall add the function *setprdim* to the module GRPACK.C. You might wonder why not simply abolish the old values 10.0 and 7.0 and always use the new values of *x_max* and *y_max* instead. One reason is that these new values do not produce nice pictures on the screen. If we call *setprdim* in a graphics program, circles will appear as ellipses on the screen, but only the printed copies will be perfect circles. So if you have no matrix printer, or if your application requires correct dimensions on the screen rather than on the printer, you should not call *setprdim,* and the pictures on the screen will be as before. Another aspect is that it is sometimes desirable to think in absolute dimensions, say, in inches, rather than in more abstract quantities such as *x_max* and *y_max,* whose values depend on the graphics adapter type.

In accordance with the title of this section, we shall now discuss how a circle can be printed. Program CIRPRINT.C assumes that a function to display a circle is given. We deal with the implementation of this function shortly. The main program finds out how large the radius *R* can be so that the circle still fits into the boundaries of the screen.

```
/* CIRPRINT.C: This program prints a large circle.    */
main()
{ extern float x_max, y_max;
  extern int X__max, Y__max;
  float xC, yC, r;
  char ch;
  printf("Is the printer ready? (Y/N): "); ch = getche();
  if (ch != 'y' && ch != 'Y') exit(1);
  setprdim();                              /* Set print dimensions */
  xC = 0.5 * x_max; yC = 0.5 * y_max;   /* Center of the circle */
  r = xC > yC ? yC : xC;                   /* Take r as large as possible */
  initgr();
  circle(xC, yC, r);   printgr(0, X__max, 0, Y__max);
  endgr();
}
```

We shall add a function named *circle* to the module GRPACK.C, so by compiling CIRPRINT.C and linking the object module together with GRPACK.OBJ, we obtain a complete executable program CIRPRINT.EXE.

As a consequence of the call *setprdim( ),* this program displays an ellipse on the screen but prints a circle. If we measure the diameter of the latter, we find that it is either 4.83 or 2.78 inch (in two decimals), depending on whether a monochrome or a color graphics adapter is used. These numbers are equal to *y_max,* see also Table 4.1.

Notice that if some program has graphics output on the screen only and is used in combination with program PRGR as a 'postprocessor', then it is the former program (not PRGR) that has to call *setprdim* to take care that eventually the graphics results will be printed with the correct dimensions.

We shall now develop the function used in CIRPRINT.C to draw a circle. Since

Table 4.1   Maximum coordinate values (after calling *setprdim*)

	Monochrome graphics adapter	Color graphics adapter
$X\_\_max$	719	639
$Y\_\_max$	347	199
$x\_max = (X\_\_max + 1)/120.0$	6.00 inch	5.33 inch
$y\_max = (Y\_\_max + 1)/72.0$	4.83 inch	2.78 inch

we can only draw straight line segments, we approximate a circle by an inscribed regular polygon. We shall use a polygon with 80 vertices, which is sufficient to make it look like a circle. The following version is simple but rather inefficient:

```
#include "math.h"
circle(xC, yC, r) float xC, yC, r;
/* This is only a preliminary version */
{ int i;
  float delta, theta;
  delta = atan(1.0)/10;    /*   80 * delta  =  2 * pi   */
  move(xC+r, yC);
  for (i=1; i <= 80; i++)
  { theta = i * delta;
    draw(xC + r * cos(theta), yC + r * sin(theta));
  }
}
```

Especially on most microcomputers, floating-point computations are rather slow. It is a good idea to use integers wherever possible, and, in particular, not to call mathematical functions such as *atan, cos, sin,* if this can be avoided. We had a similar discussion in Section 2.2, where we developed Bresenham's algorithm for straight lines. There is also a Bresenham algorithm for circles. However, this assumes that the pixel density in the horizontal direction is the same as for the vertical direction, which for the IBM PC is not the case. Yet we shall speed up the above version considerably. We shall not fully abstain from floating-point arithmetic, but simply reduce it, and use none of the mathematical functions *atan, cos, sin.* In the above version, we could have written:

```
...
theta = 0.0;
for (i=1; i <= 80; i++)
{ theta = theta + delta;
...
```

In itself this is not an improvement, since it is not likely to be much faster, and we have the disadvantage of cumulating round-off errors. (The latter is not a serious problem here, especially not if we use type *double* instead of *float* for the variables *delta* and *theta*.) The idea of repeatedly incrementing *theta* by *delta* is useful, however. We do not need the actual angle θ but rather the cosine and the sine of this angle. This means that we can benefit from the well-known goniometric relations

$$\cos (\theta + \delta) = \cos \theta \cos \delta - \sin \theta \sin \delta$$
$$\sin (\theta + \delta) = \sin \theta \cos \delta + \cos \theta \sin \delta$$

We use the same value of *delta* as above, and here, too, we need only its cosine and sine, which are constants that can be written directly in their numeric forms. We begin with *theta* = 0, so the cosine and the sine of this initial angle are 1 and 0. All other cosine and sine values can then be computed according to these two goniometric formulae for the sum of two angles. We shall convert real horizontal and vertical distances (in inches) to integer pixel-coordinate differences H and V as soon as possible, and directly use the function *draw_line,* which has (integer) pixel coordinates as arguments. Another improvement is obtained by performing the remaining floating-point computations only for one quadrant, that is, in 20 steps instead of 80. The coordinates of points in the other three quadrants can easily be derived from those of the first quadrant:

```
circle(xC, yC, r) float xC, yC, r;
/* Display a circle with given center and radius. */
/* (improved version)                             */
{ extern float horfact, vertfact;       /*  defined in GRPACK  */
  double cosd, sind, costh, sinth, c0, s0;
  int i, XC, YC, H, H0, V, V0;          /*  delta = pi / 40    */
  cosd = 0.996917333733120;             /*  cosd = cos delta   */
  sind = 0.078459095727844;             /*  sind = sin delta   */
  costh = 1.0; H = (int)(r * horfact + 0.5);
  sinth = 0.0; V = 0;                   /*  theta = i * delta  */
  XC = IX(xC); YC = IY(yC);             /*  costh = cos theta  */
  for (i=1; i<=20; i++)                 /*  sinth = sin theta  */
  { c0 = costh; s0 = sinth; H0 = H; V0 = V;
    costh = c0 * cosd - s0 * sind;
    sinth = s0 * cosd + c0 * sind;
    H = (int)(r * costh * horfact + 0.5);
    V = (int)(r * sinth * vertfact + 0.5);
    draw_line(XC+H0, YC+V0, XC+H, YC+V);
    draw_line(XC-H0, YC+V0, XC-H, YC+V);
    draw_line(XC+H0, YC-V0, XC+H, YC-V);
    draw_line(XC-H0, YC-V0, XC-H, YC-V);
  }
}
```

This improved version is larger than the preliminary one, so you might expect that the resulting executable program will take more memory. Fortunately, that need not be the case. The improved version does not use any mathematical standard functions, and therefore if we do not use these in our program for other purposes, the resulting executable version will even be much shorter than with the preliminary version. I experienced a reduction of about 4000 bytes! In connection with this, note that in the preliminary version we used # *include "math.h"*, which we do not need now. We shall include the improved version of the function *circle* in GRPACK.C.

4.5 PROGRAM TEXT OF GRPACK.C

In Chapter 3 and in this chapter we have developed a set of graphics functions, called GRPACK.C. Its predecessor was LINDRAW.C, listed in Section 2.10. These two modules are 'upwards compatible', which means that all facilities offered by LINDRAW.C are also offered by GRPACK.C. It is now time to show a listing of the latter module, and preferably the final one, since a succession of updated versions might be confusing. This is why we already include something that we shall discuss only in Chapter 5. It is placed at the end of the program text and indicated by a comment, but you can simply ignore it at this moment. The new functions of

GRPACK.C, discussed in Chapters 3 and 4, are:

clearpage, pixlit, fill, pixfill, prchar, printgr, setgrcon, setprdim, circle.

Some functions, such as *initgr*, and *dot* have been modified, but they can still be used in the same way as their predecessors in LINDRAW.C. In *initmongr*, we have added a simple feature to avoid clearing the graphics page if it should be called for the second time. We shall use this in Chapter 6.

For the benefit of programmers who simply want to use the functions of GRPACK without bothering about their implementation, there is a summary in Appendix A of this book.

```
/* GRPACK.C: An extended graphics package, by Leendert Ammeraal */
#include "dos.h"
union REGS regs;
unsigned int _STACK = 15000;
int in_textmode=1, colorgr, X__max, Y__max, drawmode=1;
static int c1, c2, c3, old_vid_state, X1, Y1, offset;

float x_max=10.0, y_max=7.0, horfact, vertfact;
static char
    lastchar,
    gtable[12] = {53, 45, 46,  7, 91, 2, 87, 87, 2,  3,  0,  0},
    ttable[12] = {97, 80, 82, 15, 25, 6, 25, 25, 2, 13, 11, 12},
    zeros[128]; /* implicitly initialized to zero */

int IX(x) float x; { return (int)(x*horfact+0.5); }
int IY(y) float y; { return Y__max-(int)(y*vertfact+0.5); }

initgr()   /* Initialize graphics */
{ int brfun();
  if (!in_textmode) error("initgr is called in graphics mode");
  colorgr = iscolor();
  if (colorgr < 0) error("Wrong display adapter");
  onbreak(brfun);              /* Set break trap */
  if (colorgr) initcolgr(); else initmongr();
  setgrcon(colorgr);
  in_textmode=0;
  horfact = X__max/x_max; vertfact = Y__max/y_max;
}

initcolgr()   /* Switch to graphics mode (color graphics) */
{ regs.h.ah = 15; /* Inquire current video state */
  int86(0x10, &regs, &regs);
  old_vid_state = regs.h.al;

  regs.h.ah = 0;   /* Set graphics mode       */
  regs.h.al = 6;   /* 640 x 200, black/white  */
  int86(0x10, &regs, &regs);
}

initmongr() /* Switch to graphics mode (monochrome graphics) */
{ static int firstcall=1;
  int i;                  /* See Section 2.6   */
/*  outp(0x3BF, 3);   Step 1, already dealt with in  iscolor */
  outp(0x3B8, 0x82);           /* Step 2 */

  for (i=0; i<12; i++)
  { outp(0x3B4, i);
    outp(0x3B5, gtable[i]);    /* Step 3 */
  }
```

```
      if (firstcall) { firstcall=0; clearpage(); }
                                      /* Step 4 */

    outp(0x3B8, 0x8A);                /* Step 5 */
  }

  setgrcon(colorgr) int colorgr; /* Set graphics constants */
  { if (colorgr)
    { X__max = 639; Y__max = 199;
      c1 = 1; c2 = 80; c3 = 1;
    } else
    { X__max = 719; Y__max = 347;
      c1 = 3; c2 = 90; c3 = 2;
    }
  }

  endgr()
  /* Wait until any key is hit and revert to text mode  */
  { getch();
    to_text();
  }

  to_text()
  /* Revert to text mode */
  { if (in_textmode) error("endgr or to_text is called in text mode");
    if (colorgr) endcolgr(); else endmongr();
    in_textmode = 1;
    onbreak(0);  /* Restore default break interrupt handler */
  }

  endcolgr()
  /* Revert to text mode (color graphics): */
  { regs.h.ah = 0; regs.h.al = old_vid_state;
    int86(0x10, &regs, &regs);
  }

  endmongr()
  /* Revert to text mode (monochrome graphics): */
  { int i, j;                                        /* See Section 2.7 */
    outp(0x3B8, 0);                                  /* Step 1 */
    for (i=0; i<12; i++)
    { outp(0x3B4, i);                                /* Step 2 */
      outp(0x3B5, ttable[i]);
    }
    for (j=0; j<256; j++) poke(0xB000, j << 4,       /* Step 3 */
      "\40\7\40\7\40\7\40\7\40\7\40\7\40\7\40\7", 16);
    outp(0x3B8, 0x08);                               /* Step 4 */
  }

  static error(str) char *str;
  /* Display a message and terminate program execution */
  { if (!in_textmode) to_text();
    printf("%s\n", str); exit(1);
  }


  move(x, y) double x, y;
  /* Move the current point to (x, y);
     x and y are screen coordinates  */
  { X1 = IX(x); Y1 = IY(y); check(X1, Y1);
  }


  draw(x, y) double x, y;
  /* Draw a line segment from the current point to  (x, y) */
  { int X2, Y2;
    X2 = IX(x); Y2 = IY(y); check(X2, Y2);
    draw_line(X1, Y1, X2, Y2);
    X1 = X2; Y1 = Y2;
  }
```

```
draw_line(X1, Y1, X2, Y2) int X1, Y1, X2, Y2;
/* Draw the line segment from (X1, Y1) to (X2, Y2);
   X1, Y1, X2, Y2 are pixel coordinates  */
{ int X, Y, T, E, dX, dY, denom, Xinc = 1, Yinc = 1,
  vertlonger = 0, aux;
  checkbreak();              /* To make DOS check for console break */
  if (in_textmode) error("Not in graphics mode (call initgr)");
  dX = X2 - X1; dY = Y2 - Y1;
  if (dX < 0) {Xinc = -1; dX = -dX;}
  if (dY < 0) {Yinc = -1; dY = -dY;}
  if (dY > dX) { vertlonger = 1; aux = dX; dX = dY; dY = aux; }
  denom = dX << 1;
  T = dY << 1;
  E = -dX; X = X1;
  Y = Y1;
  while (dX-- >= 0)
  { dot(X, Y);
    if ((E += T) > 0)
    { if (vertlonger) X += Xinc; else Y += Yinc;
      E -= denom;
    }
    if (vertlonger) Y += Yinc; else X += Xinc;
  }
  if (drawmode == 0) dot(X1, Y1);
}

checkbreak()
{ char ch;
  if (kbhit()) { ch = getch(); kbhit(); ungetch(ch); }
}

dot(X, Y) int X, Y;  /* Light or darken a pixel */
{ int pattern;
  offset= 0x2000*(Y&c1) + c2*(Y>>c3) + (X>>3);
  peek(0xB800, offset, &lastchar, 1);
  pattern = 0x80 >> (X&7);
  if (drawmode == 1) lastchar |= pattern; else
  if (drawmode == -1) lastchar &= (~pattern); else lastchar ^= pattern;
  poke(0xB800, offset, &lastchar, 1);
}

int pixlit(X, Y) int X, Y;  /* Inquire if pixel (X, Y) is lit */
{ int pattern;
  offset= 0x2000*(Y&c1) + c2*(Y>>c3) + (X>>3);
  /* c1, c2 and c3 have been defined in initgr: */
  pattern = 0x80 >> (X&7);
  peek(0xB800, offset, &lastchar, 1);
  return ((lastchar & pattern) != 0);
}

clearpage()  /* Clear the screen */
{ int i, n;
  n=(colorgr ? 128 : 256);
  for (i=0; i<n; i++) poke(0xB800, i << 7, zeros, 128);
}

int iscolor()     /* Find out which adapter is used */
{ char ch0, ch1, x;
  int86(0x11, &regs, &regs);
  if ((regs.x.ax & 0x30) != 0x30) return 1;   /* Color graphics      */
  outp(0x3BF, 3);                   /* Configuration switch, see Section 2.6 */
  peek(0xB800, 0, &ch0, 1);    /* Try to read ch0 from screen memory  */
  ch1 = ch0 ^ 0xFF;            /* Find some value different from  ch0 */
  poke(0xB800, 0, &ch1, 1);    /* Try to write this into screen memory */
  peek(0xB800, 0, &x, 1);      /* Try to read the latter value        */
  poke(0xB800, 0, &ch0, 1);    /* Restore the old value  ch0          */
  return ( x == ch1 ? 0 : -1);/* Has written value been read?         */
}
```

```
fatal()
/* Draw a diagonal, then wait until a key is pressed, and
   finally revert to text mode                            */
{ draw_line(0, Y__max,  X__max, 0); endgr();
}


check(X, Y) int X, Y;
/* If point (X, Y) lies outside the screen boundaries, then
   call fatal, print the wrong coordinates, and stop      */
{ if (X < 0 || X > X__max || Y < 0 || Y > Y__max)
  { fatal();
    printf("Point outside screen (X and Y are pixel coordinates):\n");
    printf("X = %d        Y = %d\n", X, Y);
    printf("x = %10.3f    y = %10.3f\n",
    X/horfact, (Y__max-Y)/vertfact);
    exit(1);
  }
}


int brfun()
/* Used by  onbreak, to specify what to do with a console break */
{ to_text(); exit(1); /* Before exit, return to text mode! */
}


fill(x, y) float x, y;
/* Fill a closed area, starting in point (x, y) */
/* x and y are screen coordinates, in inches     */
{ pixfill(IX(x), IY(y));
}


pixfill(X, Y) int X, Y;
  /* Fill a closed region, starting in point (X, Y) */
{ int Xleft, Xright, YY, i, dm;
  char ones=0xFF;
  dm=drawmode; drawmode=1;
  check(X, Y);
  checkbreak();      /* To make DOS check for console break */
  /* Light as many pixels as possible on line Y,
     and determine Xleft and Xright:              */
  Xleft=Xright=X;
  while (pixlit(Xleft, Y) == 0 && Xleft >= 0)
  { if (lastchar == 0)
    { poke(0xB800, offset, &ones, 1);
      Xleft &= 0xFFF8;
      if (Xright == X) Xright |= 7;
    } else dot(Xleft, Y);
    Xleft--;
  }
  Xright++;
  while (pixlit(Xright, Y) == 0 && Xright <= X__max)
  { if (lastchar == 0)
    { poke(0xB800, offset, &ones, 1);
      Xright |= 7;
    } else dot(Xright, Y);
    Xright++;
  }

  /* Recursive calls of pixfill for at most two remote points: */
  X = (Xleft+Xright) >> 1;
  for (i=-1; i <= 1; i += 2)
  { YY=Y+i;
    while (pixlit(X, YY) == 0) YY += i;
    YY = (Y+YY) >> 1;
    if (pixlit(X, YY) == 0) pixfill(X, YY);
  }
```

```
/* Recursive calls for all dark pixels next to line Y
   (with X values between Xleft and Xright):               */
for (YY=Y-1; YY<=Y+1; YY+=2)
{ X=Xleft+1;
  while (X < Xright)
  { i=pixlit(X, YY);
    if (lastchar == ones) X |= 7; else
    if (i == 0) pixfill(X, YY);
    X++;
  }
  }
  drawmode=dm;
}


prchar(ch) char ch;      /* Send byte ch to parallel printer port */
{ regs.x.dx=0;           /* Printer selection                     */
  regs.h.ah=0;           /* Send byte from AL to printer          */
  regs.h.al=ch;          /* Byte to be sent to printer            */
  int86(0x17, &regs, &regs);
}

printgr(Xlo, Xhi, Ylo, Yhi) int Xlo, Xhi, Ylo, Yhi;
/* Print contents of rectangle on matrix printer */
{ int n1, n2, ncols, i, X, Y, val;
  prchar(27); prchar('1'); /* Line spacing 7/72 inch */
  ncols=Xhi-Xlo+1;
  n1=ncols%256; n2=ncols/256;
  for (i=Ylo; i<=Yhi; i+=7)
  { checkbreak();         /* To make DOS check for console break */
    prchar(27); prchar('L'); prchar(n1); prchar(n2);
    for (X=Xlo; X<=Xhi; X++)
    { val=0;
      for (Y=i; Y<i+7; Y++)
      { val <<= 1; val |= (Y>Yhi ? 0 : pixlit(X, Y));
      }
      prchar(val);
    }
    prchar('\n');
  }
  prchar(27); prchar('@');
}


setprdim()
/* This function sets x_max and y_max such that graphics
   results will eventually be printed with correct
   dimensions, both horizontally and vertically */
{ extern float x_max, y_max;
  extern int X__max, Y__max;
  setgrcon(iscolor());
  x_max = (X__max + 1)/120.0; y_max=(Y__max + 1)/72.0;
}


/* The following program text will be discussed in Chapter 5. */

#define NASCII 128
char chlist[NASCII][11]=
{
  {0}, {0}, {0}, {0}, {0}, {0}, {0}, {0}, {0}, {0}, {0},
  {0}, {0}, {0}, {0}, {0}, {0}, {0}, {0}, {0}, {0}, {0},
  {0}, {0}, {0}, {0}, {0}, {0}, {0}, {0}, {0},
/*  */ {0},
/*!*/ {0x10, 0x38, 0x38, 0x38, 0x10, 0x10, 0x10, 0, 0x10},
/*"*/ {0x48, 0x48, 0x48},
/*#*/ {0x24, 0x24, 0x64, 0xFE, 0x44, 0xFE, 0x4C, 0x48, 0x48},
/*$*/ {0x10, 0x7C, 0xD0, 0xD0, 0x7C, 0x16, 0x16, 0x7C, 0x10},
```

```
/*%*/ {0xC2, 0x02, 0x04, 0x08, 0x10, 0x20, 0x40, 0x80, 0x86},
/*&*/ {0x30, 0x48, 0x48, 0x30, 0x50, 0x92, 0x8A, 0x8C, 0x72},
/*'*/ {0x18, 0x18, 0x18, 0x10},
/*(*/ {0x08, 0x10, 0x20, 0x20, 0x20, 0x20, 0x20, 0x10, 0x08},
/*)*/ {0x40, 0x20, 0x10, 0x10, 0x10, 0x10, 0x10, 0x20, 0x40},
/***/ {0, 0x82, 0x44, 0x28, 0xFE, 0x28, 0x44, 0x82},
/*+*/ {0, 0x10, 0x10, 0x10, 0xFE, 0x10, 0x10, 0x10},
/*,*/ {0, 0, 0, 0, 0, 0, 0x30, 0x30, 0x10, 0x20},
/*-*/ {0, 0, 0, 0, 0xFE},
/*.*/ {0, 0, 0, 0, 0, 0, 0, 0x30, 0x30},
/*/*/ {0, 0x02, 0x04, 0x08, 0x10, 0x20, 0x40, 0x80},
/*0*/ {0x38, 0x6C, 0x44, 0x44, 0x44, 0x44, 0x44, 0x6C, 0x38},
/*1*/ {0x10, 0x30, 0x50, 0x10, 0x10, 0x10, 0x10, 0x10, 0x38},
/*2*/ {0x7C, 0xC6, 0x02, 0x06, 0x18, 0x30, 0x60, 0xFE},
/*3*/ {0x7C, 0xC6, 0x02, 0x06, 0x0C, 0x06, 0x02, 0xC6, 0x7C},
/*4*/ {0x04, 0x0C, 0x1C, 0x34, 0x64, 0xC4, 0xFE, 0x04, 0x04},
/*5*/ {0xFE, 0x80, 0x80, 0xFC, 0x06, 0x02, 0x02, 0xC6, 0x7C},
/*6*/ {0x7C, 0xC6, 0x80, 0xFC, 0xC6, 0x82, 0x82, 0xC6, 0x7C},
/*7*/ {0xFE, 0x02, 0x06, 0x0C, 0x18, 0x30, 0x60, 0xC0, 0x80},
/*8*/ {0x7C, 0xC6, 0x82, 0xC6, 0x7C, 0xC6, 0x82, 0xC6, 0x7C},
/*9*/ {0x7C, 0xC6, 0x82, 0xC2, 0x7E, 0x02, 0x02, 0x06, 0x7C},
/*:*/ {0, 0x30, 0x30, 0, 0, 0, 0, 0x30, 0x30},
/*;*/ {0, 0, 0x30, 0x30, 0, 0, 0, 0x30, 0x30, 0x10, 0x20},
/*<*/ {0x04, 0x08, 0x10, 0x20, 0x40, 0x20, 0x10, 0x08, 0x04},
/*=*/ {0, 0, 0, 0, 0xFC, 0, 0, 0xFC},
/*>*/ {0x40, 0x20, 0x10, 0x08, 0x04, 0x08, 0x10, 0x20, 0x40},
/*?*/ {0x78, 0xCC, 0x84, 0x0C, 0x18, 0x10, 0x10, 0, 0x10},
/*@*/ {0x7C, 0xC6, 0x8E, 0x92, 0x92, 0x92, 0x8C, 0xC0, 0x7C},
/*A*/ {0x10, 0x38, 0x6C, 0xC6, 0x82, 0x82, 0xFE, 0x82, 0x82},
/*B*/ {0xFC, 0x86, 0x82, 0x86, 0xFC, 0x86, 0x82, 0x86, 0xFC},
/*C*/ {0x7C, 0xC6, 0x80, 0x80, 0x80, 0x80, 0x80, 0xC6, 0x7C},
/*D*/ {0xFC, 0x86, 0x82, 0x82, 0x82, 0x82, 0x82, 0x86, 0xFC},
/*E*/ {0xFE, 0x80, 0x80, 0x80, 0xF8, 0x80, 0x80, 0x80, 0xFE},
/*F*/ {0xFE, 0x80, 0x80, 0x80, 0xFC, 0x80, 0x80, 0x80, 0x80},
/*G*/ {0x7C, 0xC6, 0x82, 0x80, 0x80, 0x8E, 0x82, 0xC6, 0x7C},
/*H*/ {0x82, 0x82, 0x82, 0x82, 0xFE, 0x82, 0x82, 0x82, 0x82},
/*I*/ {0x38, 0x10, 0x10, 0x10, 0x10, 0x10, 0x10, 0x10, 0x38},
/*J*/ {0x02, 0x02, 0x02, 0x02, 0x02, 0x02, 0x02, 0xC6, 0x7C},
/*K*/ {0x86, 0x8C, 0x98, 0xB0, 0xE0, 0xB0, 0x98, 0x8C, 0x86},
/*L*/ {0x80, 0x80, 0x80, 0x80, 0x80, 0x80, 0x80, 0x80, 0xFE},
/*M*/ {0x82, 0xC6, 0xEE, 0xBA, 0x92, 0x82, 0x82, 0x82, 0x82},
/*N*/ {0x82, 0xC2, 0xE2, 0xA2, 0xB2, 0x9A, 0x8E, 0x86, 0x82},
/*O*/ {0x7C, 0xC6, 0x82, 0x82, 0x82, 0x82, 0x82, 0xC6, 0x7C},
/*P*/ {0xFC, 0x86, 0x82, 0x86, 0xFC, 0x80, 0x80, 0x80, 0x80},
/*Q*/ {0x7C, 0xC6, 0x82, 0x82, 0x82, 0x82, 0x92, 0xD6, 0x7C, 0x08, 0x08},
/*R*/ {0xFC, 0x86, 0x82, 0x86, 0xFC, 0x90, 0x98, 0x8C, 0x86},
/*S*/ {0x7C, 0xC6, 0x80, 0xC0, 0x7C, 0x06, 0x02, 0xC6, 0x7C},
/*T*/ {0xFE, 0x10, 0x10, 0x10, 0x10, 0x10, 0x10, 0x10, 0x10},
/*U*/ {0x82, 0x82, 0x82, 0x82, 0x82, 0x82, 0x82, 0xC6, 0x7C},
/*V*/ {0x82, 0x82, 0x82, 0xC6, 0x44, 0x6C, 0x28, 0x38, 0x10},
/*W*/ {0x82, 0x82, 0x82, 0x92, 0x92, 0xBA, 0xEE, 0x6C, 0x44},
/*X*/ {0xC6, 0x44, 0x6C, 0x28, 0x38, 0x28, 0x6C, 0x44, 0xC6},
/*Y*/ {0x82, 0x82, 0xC6, 0x6C, 0x38, 0x10, 0x10, 0x10, 0x10},
/*Z*/ {0xFE, 0x04, 0x0C, 0x18, 0x10, 0x30, 0x60, 0x40, 0xFE},
/*[*/ {0x7C, 0x40, 0x40, 0x40, 0x40, 0x40, 0x40, 0x40, 0x7C},
/*\*/ {0, 0x80, 0x40, 0x20, 0x10, 0x08, 0x04, 0x02},
/*]*/ {0x78, 0x08, 0x08, 0x08, 0x08, 0x08, 0x08, 0x08, 0x78},
/*^*/ {0x10, 0x28, 0x44, 0x82},
/*_*/ {0, 0, 0, 0, 0, 0, 0, 0, 0xFE},
/*`*/ {0x40, 0x20, 0x10, 0x08},
/*a*/ {0, 0, 0, 0x7C, 0x06, 0x7E, 0xC2, 0xC2, 0x7E},
/*b*/ {0x80, 0x80, 0x80, 0xFC, 0x86, 0x82, 0x82, 0x86, 0xFC},
/*c*/ {0, 0, 0, 0x7C, 0xC6, 0x80, 0x80, 0xC6, 0x7C},
/*d*/ {0x04, 0x04, 0x04, 0x7C, 0xC4, 0x84, 0x84, 0xC4, 0x7C},
/*e*/ {0, 0, 0, 0x7C, 0xC6, 0xFE, 0x80, 0xC0, 0x7C},
/*f*/ {0x1C, 0x30, 0x20, 0xFC, 0x20, 0x20, 0x20, 0x20, 0x20},
```

```
/*g*/ {0, 0, 0, 0x7A, 0xCE, 0x82, 0x82, 0xC2, 0x7E, 0x06, 0x7C},
/*h*/ {0x80, 0x80, 0x80, 0xFC, 0xC6, 0x82, 0x82, 0x82, 0x82},
/*i*/ {0, 0x30, 0, 0x30, 0x10, 0x10, 0x10, 0x10, 0x38},
/*j*/ {0, 0x0C, 0, 0x0C, 0x04, 0x04, 0x04, 0x04, 0x04, 0xCC, 0x78},
/*k*/ {0x40, 0x40, 0x40, 0x46, 0x4C, 0x78, 0x58, 0x4C, 0x46},
/*l*/ {0x30, 0x10, 0x10, 0x10, 0x10, 0x10, 0x10, 0x10, 0x38},
/*m*/ {0, 0, 0, 0xEC, 0x92, 0x92, 0x92, 0x92, 0x92},
/*n*/ {0, 0, 0, 0xBC, 0xC6, 0x82, 0x82, 0x82, 0x82},
/*o*/ {0, 0, 0, 0x7C, 0xC6, 0x82, 0x82, 0xC6, 0x7C},
/*p*/ {0, 0, 0, 0xFC, 0x86, 0x82, 0x82, 0x86, 0xFC, 0x80, 0x80},
/*q*/ {0, 0, 0, 0x7C, 0xC4, 0x84, 0x84, 0xC4, 0x7C, 0x04, 0x06},
/*r*/ {0, 0, 0, 0xBC, 0xE6, 0x80, 0x80, 0x80, 0x80},
/*s*/ {0, 0, 0, 0x7C, 0xC0, 0x7C, 0x06, 0x06, 0x7C},
/*t*/ {0, 0x40, 0x40, 0xF0, 0x40, 0x40, 0x40, 0x66, 0x3C},
/*u*/ {0, 0, 0, 0x84, 0x84, 0x84, 0x84, 0xC4, 0x7E},
/*v*/ {0, 0, 0, 0x82, 0x82, 0xC6, 0x6C, 0x38, 0x10},
/*w*/ {0, 0, 0, 0x82, 0x82, 0x92, 0xBA, 0xEE, 0x44},
/*x*/ {0, 0, 0, 0xC6, 0x6C, 0x28, 0x38, 0x6C, 0xC6},
/*y*/ {0, 0, 0, 0x82, 0x82, 0x82, 0x82, 0xC6, 0x7E, 0x06, 0x7C},
/*z*/ {0, 0, 0, 0xFE, 0x0C, 0x18, 0x30, 0x60, 0xFE},
/*{*/ {0x10, 0x20, 0x20, 0x20, 0x40, 0x20, 0x20, 0x20, 0x10},
/*|*/ {0x10, 0x10, 0x10, 0x10, 0x10, 0x10, 0x10, 0x10, 0x10},
/*}*/ {0x20, 0x10, 0x10, 0x10, 0x08, 0x10, 0x10, 0x10, 0x20},
/*~*/ {0, 0, 0, 0x60, 0x92, 0x0C},
 {0}};

textXY(X, Y, str) int X, Y; char *str;
/* Display string  str in graphics mode, starting at
   point (X, Y).                                          */
{ char *p;
  int offset, i, j, len, hpos, vpos;
  len=strlen(str);
  hpos = X>>3;
  check(8*(hpos+len), Y+10);
  for (i=0; i<len; i++)
  { p=chlist[str[i]];
    for (j=0; j<11; j++)
    { vpos=Y+j;
      offset= 0x2000*(vpos&c1) + c2*(vpos>>c3) + hpos + i;
      poke(0xB800, offset, p+j, 1);
    }
  }
}


text(str) char *str;
/* Display string  str, starting at
   the current point (X1, Y1).                            */
{ textXY(X1, Y1, str);
  X1 += strlen(str) * 8;
  check(X1, Y1);
}


imove(X, Y) int X, Y;
/* Let (X, Y) be the new current point */
{ check(X, Y); X1=X; Y1=Y;
}


idraw(X, Y) int X, Y;
/* Draw a line segment from the current point to (X, Y)  */
{ check(X, Y);
  draw_line(X1, Y1, X, Y);
  X1=X; Y1=Y;
}
```

```
circle(xC, yC, R) float xC, yC, R;
/* Display a circle with given center and radius */
{ double cosd, sind, costh, sinth, c0, s0;
    int i, XC, YC, H, H0, V, V0;              /*  delta = pi / 40   */
    cosd = 0.996917333733120;                 /*  cosd = cos delta  */
    sind = 0.078459095727844;                 /*  sind = sin delta  */
    costh = 1.0; H = (int)(R * horfact + 0.5);
    sinth = 0.0; V = 0;
    /* costh = cos theta,  sinth - sin theta,  theta = i * delta */
    XC = IX(xC); YC = IY(yC);
    if (drawmode == 0) { dot(XC+H, YC); dot(XC-H, YC); }
    for (i=1; i<=20; i++)
{ c0 = costh; s0 = sinth; H0 = H; V0 = V;
    costh = c0 * cosd - s0 * sind;
    sinth = s0 * cosd + c0 * sind;
    H = (int)(R * costh * horfact + 0.5);
    V = (int)(R * sinth * vertfact + 0.5);
    draw_line(XC+H0, YC+V0, XC+H, YC+V);
    draw_line(XC-H0, YC+V0, XC-H, YC+V);
    draw_line(XC+H0, YC-V0, XC+H, YC-V);
    draw_line(XC-H0, YC-V0, XC-H, YC-V);
}
    if (drawmode == 0) { dot(XC, YC+V); dot(XC, YC-V); }
}
```

CHAPTER 5

Writing text in graphics mode

5.1 BIT PATTERNS FOR CHARACTERS

In graphics output we often wish to include pieces of text. The PC normally produces characters by using some piece of hardware, called a character generator, but this will not work when the system is in graphics mode. However, now that we can light and darken pixels of the screen wherever we wish, it will be clear that in principle, we can produce characters on the screen ourselves. As often in software development, recognizing that in principle something can be done and actually doing it are two entirely different things. As in handwriting, we have some freedom in choosing the shape of each character, in other words, we can design our own *font*. There are three ways in which we can draw a character and display it on the screen:

(1) By drawing a number of line segments (this is the method for pen plotters).
(2) By selecting individual pixels, and setting the corresponding bits in screen memory to 1.
(3) By copying the rows of pixels of which the character is composed.

Although method (3) is less general than (1) and (2), we shall use it because of its efficiency both in space and in time. Each character (including the little blank space between two successive characters) will be eight pixels wide. This enables us to copy one byte for each row of pixels from some array to screen memory, and it will be clear that copying bytes is more efficient than copying their individual bits. We accept the two conditions imposed by this method: first, the width of each character is (a multiple of) eight pixels, and, second, that characters in screen memory can begin only at byte boundaries. We shall use eleven rows for each character, the last two of which are only used exceptionally, namely for 'descenders', such as the bottom part of the small letter g. We can then store the data for each character in an array of eleven elements. Figure 5.1 shows how the capital letter C fits into a pattern of 11×8 pixels.

We can read the eleven rows as numbers in binary representation, with the character @ for 1 and the dot for 0. For example, the top row is to be read as

$$0111\ 1100 = 0\mathrm{x}7\mathrm{C} = 124$$

Thus the data array for the letter C contains the number sequence

$$124,\ 198,\ 128,\ 128,\ 128,\ 128,\ 128,\ 198,\ 124,\ 0,\ 0$$

Though written as integers, the elements of that array will actually be of type char. Since besides the letter C there are a great many other characters, we shall use a two-dimensional array, that is, an array whose elements are in turn arrays, and

```
.@@@@@..
@@...@@.
@.......
@.......
@.......
@.......
@.......
@@...@@.
.@@@@@..
........
........
```
Fig. 5.1. The letter C

initialize it as follows:

```
static char chlist[128][11] =
{ {...,  ...,  ...,  ...,  ...,  ...,  ...,  ...,  ...,  ...,  ...},
  {...,  ...,  ...,  ...,  ...,  ...,  ...,  ...,  ...,  ...,  ...},
                            .
                            .
                            .
  {...,  ...,  ...,  ...,  ...,  ...,  ...,  ...,  ...,  ...,  ...}
};
```

where the ith sequence of the form

```
{...,  ...,  ...,  ...,  ...,  ...,  ...,  ...,  ...,  ...,  ...}
```

is the data array for the character with ASCII value i ($i = 0, \ldots, 127$). The amount of memory needed to store all character patterns is now only $128 \times 11 = 1408$ bytes.

5.2 FUNCTIONS TO WRITE TEXT IN GRAPHICS MODE

Let us assume that array *chlist* is already available (not worrying about how to obtain all the 128 data arrays; we will come to that soon). It is then rather easy to display a string of ASCII characters on the screen, starting at a given position. This starting position will be the top-left corner of the first character of the string, and we shall provide two functions, *textXY* and *text,* which differ in the way this position is given:

(1) Function *textXY* receives the (integer) pixel coordinates X and Y of the starting position as its first and second argument (the third argument being the string to be displayed).
(2) Function *text* uses the 'current point', in the same way as function *draw* would use it. In module GRPACK.C this point has the coordinates $X1$, $Y1$. After displaying the string, the new current point is the top-left corner of an imaginary new character immediately following the final character of the string. The given string is the only argument of *text.*

Most of the time we shall use the function *text* (which in turn calls *textXY*). A nice aspect of *text* is that if one string is immediately to follow another, we can simply use two successive calls of this function. For example, if the string variable *str* contains your name, and if the starting position is to be $(x0, y0)$, you can use the sequence:

```
move(x0, y0); text("My name is: "); text(str);
```

Note that $x0$ and $y0$ are real coordinates, expressed in inches. In connection with text, however, pixel coordinates are sometimes more convenient, since we know that each character appears in a box of 11×8 pixels. We now feel the need for a function similar to our function *move*, but with pixel coordinates instead of screen coordinates. We shall write this function, and, since its has integer arguments, we shall call it *imove*. For reasons of symmetry, it is then desired to have also an integer equivalent *idraw* of the well-known function *draw*. Here are these new functions:

```
textXY(X, Y, str) int X, Y; char *str;
/* Display string  str in graphics mode, starting at
    point (X, Y).                                       */
{ char *p;
  int offset, i, j, len, hpos, vpos;
  len=strlen(str);
  hpos = X>>3;
  check(8*(hpos+len), Y+10);
  for (i=0; i<len; i++)
  { p=chlist[str[i]];
    for (j=0; j<11; j++)
    { vpos=Y+j;
      offset= 0x2000*(vpos&c1) + c2*(vpos>>c3) + hpos + i;
      poke(0xB800, offset, p+j, 1);
    }
  }
}


text(str) char *str;
/* Display string  str, starting at
    the current point (X1, Y1).                         */
{ textXY(X1, Y1, str);
  X1 += strlen(str) * 8;
  check(X1, Y1);
}


imove(X, Y) int X, Y;
/* Let (X, Y) be the new current point */
{ check(X, Y); X1=X; Y1=Y;
}


idraw(X, Y) int X, Y;
/* Draw a line segment from the current point to (X, Y)   */
{ check(X, Y);
  draw_line(X1, Y1, X, Y);
  X1=X; Y1=Y;
}
```

They have already been included in GRPACK.C, listed at the end of Chapter 4. Function *text* calls *textXY*, and then updates the coordinates $X1$ and $Y1$ of the 'current point'. Since, apart from displaying text, it changes the current point $(X1, Y1)$ in the same way as, for example, the function *move* does, and since the latter functions checks whether the new current point lies inside the screen boundaries, it is reasonable that *text* also performs such a check. Function *textXY* performs the actual task of displaying the given string. The variable *len* denotes the length of the string, that is, the number of characters to be displayed. Then *hpos* is computed by shifting X three bits to the right, in other words, X is divided by 8 in the sense of integer division. The resulting value is the byte number relative to the left end of the line on the screen. The bottom-right position of the string to be displayed will have the coordinates

$$X1 = 8(hpos + len)$$
$$Y1 = Y + 10$$

so we check if this point lies within the screen boundaries. Remember that the given initial point is the top-left corner of the first character of string *str*. In the outermost loop we select the *i*th character *str*[*i*] of the given string, and use its value as a subscript for array *chlist*; since this array is two-dimensional, the array element $p = chlist[str[i]]$ is a pointer to *chlist*[*str*[*i*]][0], and, in general, $p + j$ is the address of *chlist*[*str*[*i*]][*j*], which explains the third argument in the call of *poke* ($j = 0, 1, \ldots, 10$). The *j*th row of the character has Y-coordinate $vpos = Y + j$. In Chapter 2 we have discussed how *offset* is computed, so we shall not repeat that here. The function *dot*, used so far whenever something had to be placed into screen memory, is now bypassed. We could have used it here, but that would have been much less efficient. Note that the new functions *imove* and *idraw* are useful not only in connection with text, but also if line segments are to be drawn with endpoints given in pixel coordinates. Recall that we could already draw line segments using pixel coordinates, using the function *draw_line*. However, *imove* and *idraw* use the same method as *move* and *draw*, so they are also desirable for reasons of consistency. Incidentally, though the drawn line segment is the same, there is a subtle distinction in the effects of

```
draw_line(XA, YA, XB, YB);
```

and

```
imove(XA, YA); idraw(XB, YB);
```

The call of *draw_line* leaves the current point ($X1$, $Y1$) unaffected but the calls of *imove* and *idraw* alter $X1$ and $Y1$. A similar distinction exists between

```
textXY(XA, YA, str);
```

and

```
imove(XA, YA); text(str);
```

We shall use the functions *draw_line* and *textXY* only if the coordinates $X1$ and $Y1$ must not be changed.

5.3   A DESIGN OF PRINTABLE ASCII CHARACTERS

Before we can use the new functions *text* and *textXY*, we have to take care that array *chlist* is properly initialized. For each character, we have to find eleven numbers, in the same way as such numbers were found for the letter C, using Fig. 5.1. Instead of doing this manually, we shall have it done by a program. The input data for this program will be a file, called CHARS.TXT, in which the shape of each character is defined by an 11×8 box, in the same way as Fig. 5.1 shows for the character 'C'. It is a good idea to let each box be preceded by the defined character itself. The program which reads file CHARS.TXT can then use this preceding character, to know which character it is dealing with, relieving us from the obligation to strictly follow the order of the ASCII sequence. If that program had to be as simple as possible, we should have to place all boxes below each other in a very long column, requiring a lot of paper when printed, and not suitable to be included in that form in a book. We shall therefore accept some additional program complexity in order to permit several boxes to be placed beside each other. Figure 5.2 shows the complete contents of file CHARS.TXT.

```
A               B               C               D               E               F

...@....        @@@@@@..        .@@@@@..        @@@@@@..        @@@@@@@.        @@@@@@@.
..@@@...        @....@@.        @@...@@.        @....@@.        @.......        @.......
.@@.@@..        @.....@.        @.......        @.....@.        @.......        @.......
@@...@@.        @....@@.        @.......        @.....@.        @.......        @.......
@.....@.        @@@@@@..        @.......        @.....@.        @@@@@...        @@@@@@..
@.....@.        @....@@.        @.......        @.....@.        @.......        @.......
@@@@@@@.        @.....@.        @.......        @.....@.        @.......        @.......
@.....@.        @....@@.        @@...@@.        @....@@.        @.......        @.......
@.....@.        @@@@@@..        .@@@@@..        @@@@@@..        @@@@@@@.        @.......
........        ........        ........        ........        ........        ........
........        ........        ........        ........        ........        ........

G               H               I               J               K               L

.@@@@@..        @.....@.        ..@@@...        ......@.        @....@@.        @.......
@@...@@.        @.....@.        ...@....        ......@.        @...@@..        @.......
@.....@.        @.....@.        ...@....        ......@.        @..@@...        @.......
@.......        @.....@.        ...@....        ......@.        @.@@....        @.......
@.......        @@@@@@@.        ...@....        ......@.        @@@.....        @.......
@...@@@.        @.....@.        ...@....        ......@.        @.@@....        @.......
@.....@.        @.....@.        ...@....        ......@.        @..@@...        @.......
@@...@@.        @.....@.        ...@....        @@...@@.        @...@@..        @.......
.@@@@@..        @.....@.        ..@@@...        .@@@@@..        @....@@.        @@@@@@@.
........        ........        ........        ........        ........        ........
........        ........        ........        ........        ........        ........

M               N               O               P               Q               R

@.....@.        @.....@.        .@@@@@..        @@@@@@..        .@@@@@..        @@@@@@..
@@...@@.        @@....@.        @@...@@.        @....@@.        @@...@@.        @....@@.
@@@.@@@.        @@@...@.        @.....@.        @.....@.        @.....@.        @.....@.
@.@@@.@.        @.@...@.        @.....@.        @....@@.        @.....@.        @....@@.
@..@..@.        @.@@..@.        @.....@.        @@@@@@..        @.....@.        @@@@@@..
@.....@.        @..@@.@.        @.....@.        @.......        @.....@.        @..@....
@.....@.        @...@@@.        @.....@.        @.......        @..@..@.        @...@@..
@.....@.        @....@@.        @@...@@.        @.......        @@.@.@@.        @....@@.
@.....@.        @.....@.        .@@@@@..        @.......        .@@@@@..        @....@@.
........        ........        ........        ........        ....@...        ........
........        ........        ........        ........        ....@...        ........

S               T               U               V               W               X

.@@@@@..        @@@@@@@.        @.....@.        @.....@.        @.....@.        @@...@@.
@@...@@.        ...@....        @.....@.        @.....@.        @.....@.        .@...@..
@.......        ...@....        @.....@.        @.....@.        @.....@.        .@@.@@..
@@......        ...@....        @.....@.        @@...@@.        @..@..@.        ..@.@...
.@@@@@..        ...@....        @.....@.        .@...@..        @..@..@.        ..@@@...
.....@@.        ...@....        @.....@.        .@@.@@..        @.@@@.@.        ..@.@...
......@.        ...@....        @.....@.        ..@.@...        @@@.@@@.        .@@.@@..
@@...@@.        ...@....        @@...@@.        ..@@@...        .@@.@@..        .@...@..
.@@@@@..        ...@....        .@@@@@..        ...@....        .@...@..        @@...@@.
........        ........        ........        ........        ........        ........
........        ........        ........        ........        ........        ........
```

Fig. 5.2. Contents of the file CHARS.TXT

```
   Y          Z          a          b          c          d

@.....@.   @@@@@@@.   ........   @.......   ........   .....@..
@.....@.   .....@..   ........   @.......   ........   .....@..
@@...@@.   ....@...   ........   @.......   ........   .....@..
.@@.@@..   ...@@...   .@@@@@..   @@@@@@..   .@@@@@..   .@@@@@..
..@@@...   ...@....   ......@@   @....@@.   @@...@@.   @@...@.
...@....   ..@@....   .@@@@@@@   @.....@.   @.......   @.....@.
...@....   .@@.....   @@....@.   @.....@.   @.......   @.....@.
...@....   .@......   @@...@@.   @....@@.   @@...@@.   @@...@.
...@....   @@@@@@@.   .@@@@@@@   @@@@@@..   .@@@@@..   .@@@@@..
........   ........   ........   ........   ........   ........
........   ........   ........   ........   ........   ........


   e          f          g          h          i          j

........   ...@@@..   ........   @.......   ........   .......
........   ..@@....   ........   @.......   ..@@....   ....@@..
........   ..@.....   ........   @.......   ..@@....   ....@@..
.@@@@@..   @@@@@@..   .@@@@.@.   @@@@@@..   ...@....   ....@..
@@...@@.   ..@.....   @@..@@@.   @@...@@.   ...@....   ....@..
@@@@@@@.   ..@.....   @.....@.   @.....@.   ...@....   ....@..
@.......   ..@.....   @.....@.   @.....@.   ...@....   ....@..
@@......   ..@.....   @@....@.   @.....@.   ...@....   ....@..
.@@@@@..   ..@.....   .@@@@@@.   @.....@.   ..@@@...   ....@..
........   ........   ......@@   ........   ........   @@..@@..
........   ........   .@@@@@..   ........   ........   .@@@@...


   k          l          m          n          o          p

.@......   ..@@....   ........   ........   ........   .......
.@......   ...@....   ........   ........   ........   .......
.@......   ...@....   ........   ........   ........   .......
.@...@@.   ...@....   @@@.@@..   @.@@@@..   .@@@@@..   @@@@@@..
.@..@@..   ...@....   @..@..@.   @@...@@.   @@...@@.   @....@@.
.@@@@...   ...@....   @..@..@.   @.....@.   @.....@.   @.....@.
.@.@@...   ...@....   @..@..@.   @.....@.   @.....@.   @.....@.
.@..@@..   ...@....   @..@..@.   @.....@.   @@...@@.   @....@@.
.@...@@.   ..@@@...   @..@..@.   @.....@.   .@@@@@..   @@@@@@..
........   ........   ........   ........   ........   @.......
........   ........   ........   ........   ........   @.......


   q          r          s          t          u          v

........   ........   ........   ........   ........   .......
........   ........   ........   .@......   ........   .......
........   ........   ........   .@......   ........   .......
.@@@@@..   @.@@@@..   .@@@@@..   @@@@....   @....@..   @.....@.
@@...@..   @@@..@@.   @@......   .@......   @....@..   @.....@.
@....@..   @.......   .@@@@@..   .@......   @....@..   @@...@@.
@....@..   @.......   ....@@..   .@......   @....@..   .@@.@@..
@@...@..   @.......   .@@..@@.   .@@..@@.   @@...@..   ..@@@...
.@@@@@..   @.......   .@@@@@..   ..@@@@..   .@@@@@@.   ...@....
.....@..   ........   ........   ........   ........   .......
....@@..   ........   ........   ........   ........   .......
```

Fig. 5.2. (continued)

```
w           x           y           z           0           1

........    ........    ........    ........    ..@@@...    ...@....
........    ........    ........    ........    .@@.@@..    ..@@....
........    ........    ........    ........    .@...@..    .@.@....
@.....@.    @@...@@.    @.....@.    @@@@@@@.    .@...@..    ...@....
@.....@.    .@@.@@..    @.....@.    ....@@..    .@...@..    ...@....
@..@..@.    ..@.@...    @.....@.    ...@@...    .@...@..    ...@....
@.@@@.@.    ..@@@...    @.....@.    ..@@....    .@...@..    ...@....
@@@.@@@.    .@@.@@..    @@....@.    .@@.....    .@@.@@..    ...@....
.@...@..    @@...@@.    .@@@@@@.    @@@@@@@.    ..@@@...    ..@@@...
........    ........    .....@@.    ........    ........    ........
........    ........    .@@@@@..    ........    ........    ........


2           3           4           5           6           7

.@@@@@..    .@@@@@..    .....@..    @@@@@@@.    .@@@@@..    @@@@@@@.
@@...@@.    @@...@@.    ....@@..    @.......    @@...@@.    ......@.
......@.    ......@.    ...@@@..    @.......    @.......    .....@@.
....@@..    ....@@..    ..@@.@..    @@@@@@..    @@@@@@..    ....@@..
...@@...    ....@@..    .@@..@..    .....@@.    @@...@@.    ...@@...
..@@....    ......@.    @@...@..    ......@.    @.....@.    ..@@....
.@@.....    @@...@@.    @@@@@@@.    ......@.    @@...@@.    .@@.....
@@@@@@@.    .@@@@@..    .....@..    @@...@@.    @@...@@.    @@......
........    ........    .....@..    .@@@@@..    .@@@@@..    @.......
........    ........    ........    ........    ........    ........
........    ........    ........    ........    ........    ........


8           9           !           "           #           $

.@@@@@..    .@@@@@..    ...@....    .@..@...    ..@..@..    ...@....
@@...@@.    @@...@@.    ..@@@...    .@..@...    ..@..@..    .@@@@@..
@.....@.    @.....@.    ..@@@...    .@..@...    .@@..@..    @@.@....
@@...@@.    @@....@.    ..@@@...    ........    @@@@@@@.    @@.@....
.@@@@@..    .@@@@@@.    ...@....    ........    .@..@...    .@@@@@..
@@...@@.    ......@.    ...@....    ........    @@@@@@@.    ...@.@@.
@.....@.    ......@.    ...@....    ........    .@..@@..    ...@.@@.
@@...@@.    .....@@.    ........    ........    .@..@...    .@@@@@..
.@@@@@..    .@@@@@..    ...@....    ........    .@..@...    ...@....
........    ........    ........    ........    ........    ........
........    ........    ........    ........    ........    ........


%           &           '           (           )           *

@@....@.    ..@@....    ...@@...    ....@...    .@......    ........
......@.    .@..@...    ...@@...    ...@....    ..@.....    @.....@.
.....@..    .@..@...    ...@@...    ..@.....    ...@....    .@...@..
....@...    ..@@....    ...@....    ..@.....    ...@....    ..@.@...
...@....    .@.@....    ........    ..@.....    ...@....    @@@@@@@.
..@.....    @..@..@.    ........    ..@.....    ...@....    ..@.@...
.@......    @...@.@.    ........    ..@.....    ...@....    .@...@..
@.......    @...@@..    ........    ...@....    ..@.....    @.....@.
@....@@.    .@@@..@.    ........    ....@...    .@......    ........
........    ........    ........    ........    ........    ........
........    ........    ........    ........    ........    ........
```

Fig. 5.2. (continued)

```
    +            ,            -            .            /            :

........    ........    ........    ........    .......@.    ........
...@....    ........    ........    ........    ......@..    ..@@....
...@....    ........    ........    ........    .....@...    ..@@....
...@....    ........    ........    ........    ....@....    ........
@@@@@@.    ........    @@@@@@.    ........    ...@.....    ........
...@....    ........    ........    ........    ..@......    ........
...@....    ..@@....    ........    ..@@....    .@.......    ..@@....
........    ..@@....    ........    ..@@....    @.......    ..@@....
........    ...@....    ........    ........    ........    ........
........    ..@.....    ........    ........    ........    ........


    ;            <            =            >            ?            @

........    .....@..    ........    .@......    .@@@@...    .@@@@@..
........    ....@...    ........    ..@.....    @@..@@..    @@...@@.
..@@....    ...@....    ........    ...@....    @....@..    @....@..
..@@....    ..@.....    ........    ....@...    ....@@..    @..@..@.
........    .@......    @@@@@@.    .....@..    ...@@...    @..@..@.
........    ..@.....    ........    ....@...    ...@....    @..@..@.
..@@....    ...@....    @@@@@@.    ...@....    ........    @...@@..
..@@....    ....@...    ........    ..@.....    ...@....    @@......
...@....    .....@..    ........    .@......    ........    .@@@@@..
..@.....    ........    ........    ........    ........    ........


    [            \            ]            ^            _            '

.@@@@@..    ........    .@@@@...    ...@....    ........    .@......
.@......    @.......    ....@...    ..@.@...    ........    ..@.....
.@......    .@......    ....@...    .@...@..    ........    ...@....
.@......    ..@.....    ....@...    @.....@.    ........    ....@...
.@......    ...@....    ....@...    ........    ........    ........
.@......    ....@...    ....@...    ........    ........    ........
.@......    .....@..    ....@...    ........    ........    ........
.@......    ......@.    ....@...    ........    ........    ........
.@@@@@..    ........    .@@@@...    ........    @@@@@@@.    ........
........    ........    ........    ........    ........    ........
........    ........    ........    ........    ........    ........


    {            |            }            ~

...@....    ...@....    ..@.....    ........
..@.....    ...@....    ...@....    ........
..@.....    ...@....    ...@....    ........
..@.....    ...@....    ...@....    ........
.@......    ...@....    ....@...    .@@.....
..@.....    ...@....    ...@....    @..@..@.
..@.....    ...@....    ...@....    ....@@..
..@.....    ...@....    ...@....    ........
...@....    ...@....    ..@.....    ........
........    ........    ........    ........
........    ........    ........    ........
```

Fig. 5.2. (continued)

We shall use this file to obtain a program module of the form:

```
static char chlist[128][11] =
{ {...},
   ...
  {...}'
}
```

which we will call CHARS.C.

5.4 A PROGRAM GENERATOR FOR FONTS

We shall now develop a program, called CHARSGEN.C, which is in fact a program generator. As shown in Fig. 5.3, its input and output are the files CHARS.TXT and CHARS.C, respectively.

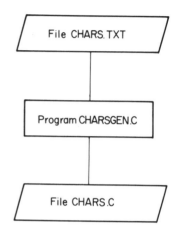

Fig. 5.3. *Program generator CHARSGEN.C*

In program CHARSGEN.C we shall first read the entire file CHARS.TXT, and collect all data in an array *chr* of 128 rows and 11 columns, identical to the array *chlist* for which the defining source code is to be generated. As discussed before, the complexity of this task is mainly due to our placing several character boxes (say, *n* of them) beside each other. In Fig. 5.2, normally $n = 6$, with the exception that at the end of the file we have $n = 4$. This follows from the fact that we have $94 = 15 \times 6 + 4$ printable ASCII characters in the file. The ASCII characters with values $0, 1, \ldots, 31$ and 127 are non-printable, and the space (value 32), though normally considered printable, need not be included either. Thus 34 characters are not in the file, and 94 are, which makes 128 characters altogether. We now have to make our program read the file CHARS.TXT, and we will do this in a purely sequential way, which means that each time *n* characters are dealt with in parallel. The array elements

$$sym[0], sym[1], \ldots, sym[n-1]$$

will contain these *n* characters themselves. They are read from the line that precedes the *n* boxes defining their shapes. After this, the eleven lines containing these boxes are read. Note that for character *sym*[0] the second row (of eight positions) can be read only when the first row has been read for all *n* characters. This is meant above by saying that *n* characters are read in parallel. Of course, we have to be careful in skipping the correct number of spaces and newline characters, but all this is not really difficult. Before we proceed, it is good to have a look at the first part of program CHARSGEN.C, that is, up to the statement *fclose(fpin)*.

```
/* CHARSGEN.C: This program reads the file CHARS.TXT, which
               displays the shapes of characters. It generates
               the program module CHARS.C, containing the
               same information in coded form.                    */

#include "stdio.h"
#define NASCII 128
FILE *fpin, *fpout;


main()
{ static unsigned char chr[NASCII][11];   /* Initialized to zero */
  unsigned char sym[10], k, ch;
  int s, i, j, h, l, ich, n, m;
  fpin = fopen("chars.txt", "r");
  if (fpin==NULL) { printf("No input file chars.txt."); exit(1); }
  while (ich=getc(fpin), ich>=0)
  { n=0;
    do
    { sym[n]=ich; n++;
      skip(10);
      ich = getc(fpin);
    } while (ich != '\n');
    /* The n characters sym[0], ..., sym[n-1] have now been read
       on one line; their tables follow!                          */
    skipnewline("at the beginning of a table");
    for (i=0; i<11; i++)
    { for (h=0; h<n; h++)
      { s=0;
        for (j=0; j<8; j++)
        { ch=getc(fpin);
          s = 2*s + (ch == '@');
        }
        chr[sym[h]][i]=s;
        skip(3);
      }
      skipnewline("within a table");
    }
    skipnewline("(first after table)");
    skipnewline("(second after table)");
  }
  fclose(fpin);

  fpout = fopen("chars.c", "w");
  fprintf(fpout, "#define NASCII 128\n");
  fprintf(fpout, "char chlist[NASCII][11]=\n{\n ");
  for (l=0; l < NASCII - 1; l++)
  { fprintf(fpout, "{");
    m=10;
    while (m>0 && chr[l][m]==0) m--;
    /* Any zero elements following chr[l][m] can be omitted */
    for (i=0; i<=m; i++)
    { k=chr[l][i];
      if (k==0) putc('0', fpout); else
        fprintf(fpout, "0x%1X%1X", k>>4, k&15);
      if (i<m) fprintf(fpout, ", ");
    }
    putc('}', fpout);
    fprintf(fpout, ", ");
    if (l == 10 || l == 21) fprintf(fpout, "\n "); else
    if (l >= 31 && l < NASCII - 2) /* Display next character: */
      fprintf(fpout, "\n/*%c*/ ", l+1);
  }
  fprintf(fpout, "\n {0}};\n");
  fclose(fpout);
}
```

```
skip(n) int n; /* Skip at most n characters of the same line */
{ int i, ch;
  for (i=0; i<n; i++)
  { ch=getc(fpin);
    if (ch=='\n') { ungetc(ch, fpin); break; }
  }
}

skipnewline(s) char *s;
 /* Skip a newline character, which must be present */
{ char ch;
  ch=getc(fpin);
  if (ch!='\n')
  { printf("Newline character expected %s", s);
  }
}
```

This program requires the input file CHARS.TXT to have exactly the correct format: a missing or an extra space or newline character will cause problems. If the program were to be used very often and by various users, it had better be improved on this point, but as an auxiliary program, to be executed only once, it will do. In C all elements of static or external arrays are guaranteed to have zero initial values unless explicitly initialized otherwise. This is relevant both to the first and the second part of the program.

After having collected all the information in array *chr*, the second part generates the program text which defines and initialized array *chlist*. Here we shall again make things a little more complex than is strictly necessary. We shall take care that the line lengths of the output is reasonable, and avoid trailing sequences of zeros. Let me give you a simple example to explain what I mean. If in C some array *A* is initialized as

```
static int A[5] = { 1, 2, 3, 0, 0 };
```

then this may be replaced with

```
static int A[5] = { 1, 2, 3 };
```

since here the final two elements of *A* are implicitly initialized to zero. Now each of the first 32 rows of array *chlist* may consist of eleven zeros (or any other values), since these rows correspond to non-printable characters, and will therefore not be used. If published in a book like this, it would be awkward if the resulting file CHARS.C began with $32 \times 11 = 352$ zero elements, so we shall abbreviate

```
{0, 0, 0, 0, 0, 0, 0 ,0, 0, 0, 0}
```

to

```
{0}
```

and place more than one of such abbreviations on the same line. Since each non-zero element of the two-dimensional array *chlist* should be interpreted as a row of eight pixels, it is nice to write them as two hexadecimal digits, preceded by the prefix 0x required by the C compiler. It is also nice to include a comment at the beginning of all lines with codes for printable characters. It is good to have a look at the actual results, the file CHARS.C, before studying the program that has produced it. You will find this piece of program text included in the module

GRPACK.C, at the end of Chapter 4. It begins with the line

```
#define NASCII 128
```

and it ends with

```
{0}};
```

Instead of including it in GRPACK.C, I could have compiled it separately, but then we would have had the awkward obligation to supply it always to the linker, even if we were not using the graphics text functions. After all, the identifier *chlist* occurs in *textXY,* and the linker would complain about an unresolved external name. Combining the graphics text functions and the array *chlist* into one file might seem the obvious solution, but then some variables could not have the storage class 'static', so the latter solution is undesirable for reasons of security. Since normally we want to include some text in graphics output, I think that array *chlist* will be used very often, and that the chosen solution is not bad at all.

After these reflections about the proper place of CHAR.C, we return to our discussion of how this file is generated. In program CHARSGEN.C, we let the variable l range from 0 to 126. The highest character value, 127, is not a printable character, nor is the corresponding program text {0} followed by a comma, so we deal with it in a special way, nearly at the end of the main program. For each value of l, that is, for each character, we find the value m, with the property that, for all values $i > m$, the array element $chr[l][i]$ is zero, and need therefore not be initialized. Thus, to obtain the values that are to be written to file CHARS.C, we let i range from 0 to m, and use the values $k = chr[l][i]$. You may have noticed some occurrences of the keyword *unsigned* in the program. Recall that in this way we prevent the 'sign bit' of characters from being extended to the left, when the characters are converted to integers. We have discussed this in Section 1.2. Note that in $k \gg 4$ and $k \& 15$ we use bit operators to obtain the two hexadecimal digits of k. As in the first part of the program, we have to pay some attention to lexical aspects, in other words, we have to write spaces, commas and braces where these are required, but we will not discuss those aspects in more detail.

Normally, the user will call only the function *text* (or *textXY*) and will not access array *chlist* directly, so it seems that we had better have added the keyword *static* to the definition of this array to prevent it from being used accidentally. However, in Section 5.6 we shall discuss a useful application of accessing array *chlist* ourselves.

5.5   A DEMONSTRATION PROGRAM

It is now time to use the tools we have made. As an example, we shall first display all the characters in the shapes we have designed ourselves. Then we shall also display some computed value, say, the square root of 2, so we now have to deal with a value given in its internal binary format. Fortunately, the C language provides a very useful function to convert any numeric value into the string that would be printed. Despite its name, this function, *sprintf*, does not perform any output action, but gives the result in a string instead. We shall also use the new functions *imove* and *idraw*. Figure 5.4 shows the output of program TEXTDEMO.C.

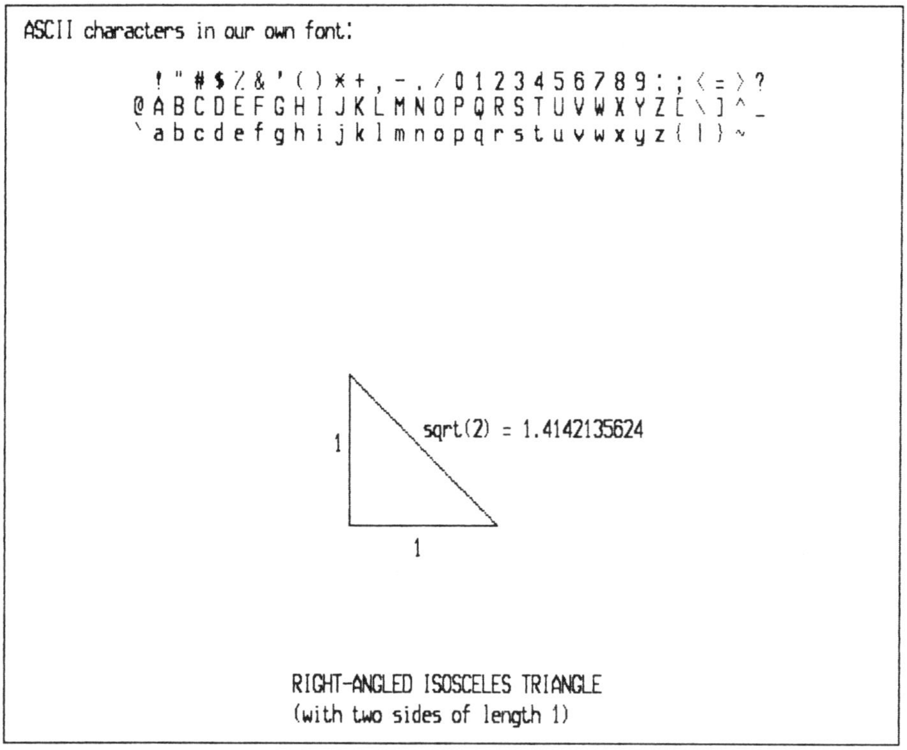

```
ASCII characters in our own font:

        ! " # $ % & ' ( ) * + , - . / 0 1 2 3 4 5 6 7 8 9 : ; < = > ?
        @ A B C D E F G H I J K L M N O P Q R S T U V W X Y Z [ \ ] ^ _
        ` a b c d e f g h i j k l m n o p q r s t u v w x y z { | } ~
```

sqrt(2) = 1.4142135624

1

1

RIGHT-ANGLED ISOSCELES TRIANGLE
(with two sides of length 1)

Fig. 5.4. Output of program TEXTDEMO.C

```
/* TEXTDEMO.C: This program displays and prints all characters
               of which the font is coded in array chlist.
               It also shows how a computed value is displayed
               and printed in graphics output.                  */
#include "math.h"

main()
{ int i;
  extern float x_max, y_max;
  extern int X__max, Y__max;
  int Xmiddle;
  float x0, y0;
  static char s[20];
  setprdim();
  s[1] = ' '; Xmiddle = (X__max + 1)/2;
  initgr();
  /* Draw the screen boundaries:  */
  imove(0, 0); idraw(X__max, 0); idraw(X__max, Y__max);
  idraw(0, Y__max); idraw(0, 0);

  /* Display the ASCII sequence:  */
  imove(16, 8);
  text("ASCII characters in our own font:");
  for (i=32; i<127; i++)
  { s[0]=i;
    if (i % 32 == 0) imove(Xmiddle - 32 * 8, 20 + i/32 * 12);
    text(s);
  }
```

```
    imove(Xmiddle - 16*8, Y__max - 32);
    text("RIGHT-ANGLED ISOSCELES TRIANGLE");
    imove(Xmiddle - 16*8, Y__max - 18);
    text( "(with two sides of length 1)");

    x0 = 0.5 * x_max - 0.7;            /* (x0, y0) is the bottom-left  */
    y0 = 0.5 * y_max - 1.0;            /* point of the triangle        */
    move(x0, y0); draw(x0 + 1.0, y0); draw(x0, y0+1.0); draw(x0, y0);
    move(x0 - 0.1, y0 + 0.6); text("1");   /* Length of vertical side  */
    move(x0 + 0.45, y0 - 0.08); text("1"); /* Horizontal side          */
    sprintf(s, "%12.10f", sqrt(2.0));
    move(x0 + 0.5, y0 + 0.7);
    text("sqrt(2) = "); text(s);           /* Side with length sqrt(2) */

    printgr(0, X__max, 0, Y__max);
    endgr();
}
```

Note that the very first 'printable' character is the space character, hence the space that precedes the exclamation mark (!) in the output. Between two successive lines of text, we can have any amount of blank space we wish, in other words, the Y-coordinate of each line can be chosen arbitrarily. Each line takes at least 11 pixels, or, on paper, 11/72 inch, but we may use other distances instead. For example, in Fig. 5.4 the line

RIGHT-ANGLED ISOSCELES TRIANGLE

is placed 14 pixels above the line

(*with two sides of length* 1)

The X-coordinates, however, are truncated to a multiple of 8 pixels. Since we have 120 dots per inch (using double density), we print $120/8 = 15$ characters per inch.

5.6 DESIGNING NEW CHARACTERS

Unlike some other variables, such as, for example, $X1$ and $Y1$, the declaration of *chlist* does not begin with the keyword *static*. This means that we have access to this array, which enables us to alter its contents. In this way, we can either change the shapes of existing characters or add new characters, without using the 'heavy' tools of program CHARSGEN.C and file CHARS.TXT. As an example, we shall add an integral sign, which is frequently used in mathematics, placing its 11 rows of 8 pixels into *chlist*[1]. First we have to design this character, which could be done as shown in Fig. 5.5.

```
.....@@.      0x06
....@.@@      0x0B
...@@...      0x18
...@@...      0x18
...@@...      0x18
...@@...      0x18
...@@...      0x18
...@@...      0x18
...@@...      0x18
@@.@....      0xD0
.@@.....      0x60     Fig. 5.5. Integral sign
```

The eleven values we need are also shown for each row of eight dots. We demonstrate the use of the newly defined character in program NEWCHAR.C, which prints a well-known formula in which the integral sign occurs twice. Since we use row 1 of the two-dimensional array *chlist*, we use the (octal) notation \001 in the string constant

```
"\001   f(x)  dx  =  -  \001   f(x)  dx"
```

to denote the integral sign. The output of program NEWCHAR.C is shown in Fig. 5.6.

$$\int_a^b f(x)\ dx = -\int_b^a f(x)\ dx$$

Fig. 5.6. Output of program NEWCHAR.C

```
/* NEWCHAR: This program uses the integral sign in its output,
           both on the screen and on the printer              */
main()
{ extern char chlist[128][11];
  static char s[11] =
  {0x06, 0x0B, 0x18, 0x18, 0x18, 0x18, 0x18, 0x18, 0x18, 0xD0, 0x60};
  int i, X0, Y0;
  for (i=0; i<11; i++) chlist[1][i] = s[i];
  setprdim();
  initgr();
  X0=200; Y0=100;
  imove(X0, Y0);
  text("\001   f(x)  dx  =  -  \001   f(x)  dx");
  imove(X0+8, Y0+9); text("a");
  imove(X0+8, Y0-11); text("b");
  imove(X0+128, Y0+9); text("b");
  imove(X0+128, Y0-11); text("a");
  printgr(0, 600, Y0-30, Y0+30);
  endgr();
}
```

CHAPTER 6

DIG: *Drawing with Interactive Graphics*

6.1 INTRODUCTION

In this chapter, we shall deal with an area where Computer Graphics is particularly useful, namely CAD. As you will probably know, the latter term stands for Computer Aided Drawing, also known as Computer Aided Design. Books on CAD are usually meant for designers, who are still using a pencil and paper and who need to be persuaded to use the computer instead. Our approach will be different. This book is meant for programmers, and this chapter is not an exception to that, so we shall deal with some internal aspects of CAD, normally not exposed to designers. We shall not discuss commercially available CAD packages, but develop an interactive graphics program of our own. I called it DIG, short for Drawing with Interactive Graphics, and although it cannot compete with other CAD programs in all respects, I think it may be useful if only small drawings or sketches are desired. In any case, it has three nice aspects:

1. It runs on any IBM PC (or a compatible machine) with a color graphics or a monochrome graphics adapter. A simple matrix printer is sufficient to obtain a hard copy of graphics output.
2. The complete source text is listed in this book, which is exceptional for a CAD program.
3. Compared with other CAD systems, it is extremely cheap, see also points 1 and 2.

6.2 CURSOR MOVEMENTS

We designate a point on the screen by means of a special symbol, called a *cursor*. The shape of the cursor is not very important, and we shall use a small rectangle for it, with one dot in the middle. We wish to be able to move the cursor anywhere on the screen. There are special devices for graphics input, such as a mouse, a graphics tablet and a light pen, but I will not rely on the willingness of all readers of this book to buy such hardware. Instead, we shall simply use the four arrow keys, located on the right-hand side of a normal keyboard, and try to develop software which makes these keys easy to use for our purposes. If you insist on using a mouse, you may find useful information in Appendix B.

The shape of our cursor is shown in Fig. 6.1.

The dot in the center of the rectangle is the point that we want to denote by the cursor. Calling its pixel coordinates *Xcur* and *Ycur,* we 'draw' the cursor using the

```
XXXXXXXXX
XX       XX
XX   X   XX
XX       XX
XXXXXXXXX
```

Fig. 6.1. Cursor

function *cur*:

```
cur()
{ int i, j, dm;
  dm = drawmode; drawmode = 0;
  for (j=-2; j<=2; j+=4)
  for (i=-4; i<=4; i++) dot(Xcur+i, Ycur+j);
  dot(Xcur-4, Ycur-1); dot(Xcur-3, Ycur-1);
  dot(Xcur+3, Ycur-1); dot(Xcur+4, Ycur-1);
  dot(Xcur-4, Ycur); dot(Xcur-3, Ycur); dot(Xcur+3, Ycur);
  dot(Xcur+4, Ycur);  dot(Xcur, Ycur);
  dot(Xcur-4, Ycur+1); dot(Xcur-3, Ycur+1);
  dot(Xcur+3, Ycur+1); dot(Xcur+4, Ycur+1);
  drawmode = dm;
}
```

Note that in the inner part of this function, we have *drawmode* = 0, which means that pixel states are 'toggled', as discussed in Section 3.1. So after calling this function twice for the same point (*Xcur, Ycur*), the screen is in the same state as before the first call. This enables us to keep any existing figure undamaged if we first place the cursor there and then remove it.

Since we want to move the cursor, we now have to deal with the four arrow keys. Curiously enough, pressing such a key causes two characters to become available, the first of which is the null character. This character consists of eight zero bits, so its value is 0, not to be confused with the character '0', whose value is 48. The value of the second character depends on the particular key that is being pressed, in the following way:

Pressed key	Value 1st char.	Value 2nd char.
↑	0	72
←	0	75
→	0	77
↓	0	80

If an arrow key is pressed, we have to move the cursor some step in the indicated direction. This is done in three steps:

1. We call the function *cur* to erase the old cursor in the position (*Xcur, Ycur*). (Recall that we use *drawmode* = 0, which 'toggles' the pixel states.)
2. We update either *Xcur* or *Ycur* according to which key has been pressed, using the current stepsize.
3. We call the function *cur* again to draw the new cursor.

We shall provide a means to alter the stepsize. Initially, the variable *stsize*, used for this purpose, is given the value 8, which means that pressing an arrow key moves the cursor only eight pixels in the given direction. Sometimes a larger stepsize is desirable. We shall use the 'greater than' character for this purpose: pressing the '>' key will have the effect that the value of *stsize* is doubled. Similarly, we halve *stsize* if the 'less than' key (<) is pressed. However, we shall not admit the stepsize to grow infinitely; let us use the value 200 as its maximum. Also, the smallest stepsize that we admit will be one pixel. Similar limitations have to be imposed on the values of *Xcur* and *Ycur* to keep the cursor within the screen boundaries. We shall actually use a window somewhat smaller than the full screen, and display some useful information as text outside this window. This concerns the keys that may be pressed, the current step size and cursor coordinates, and the message 'Invalid', which will appear if any invalid key is pressed. Note that the window also avoids problems due to the size of the cursor. For example, we cannot use the value $Xcur = 0$, since that would mean that the left half of the cursor lies to the left of pixel column $X = 0$. Besides the arrow keys and the characters '>' and '<', we shall accept the characters '*Q*' and '*q*' as valid. They will be interpreted as a 'Quit' command, so it will cause the computer to revert to text mode and to terminate program execution. Program CURSOR.C performs all this, provided that after compilation we link it together with GRPACK.OBJ.

```
/* CURSOR.C: A demonstration program for cursor movements */

extern int X__max, Y__max, drawmode;
int Xmin1, Xmax1, Ymin1, Ymax1, Ybottext, Xcur, Ycur, stsize=8;

main()
{ char ch;
  initgr();
  window();
  prnum(80, stsize);
  Xcur = Xmin1; Ycur = Ymin1; cur();
  prnum(160, Xcur); prnum(240, Ycur);
  while (ch = getch(), ch = toupper(ch), ch != 'Q')
  { message("          "); /* Clear message area */
    if (ch == 0)  /* This happens if an arrow key is pressed */
    { ch = getch();
      switch (ch)
      { case 75:
          cur(); Xcur -= stsize;
          if (Xcur < Xmin1) Xcur = Xmin1;
          cur(); prnum(160, Xcur); break; /* Left  */
        case 77:
          cur(); Xcur += stsize;
          if (Xcur > Xmax1) Xcur = Xmax1;
          cur(); prnum(160, Xcur); break; /* Right */
        case 72:
          cur(); Ycur -= stsize;
          if (Ycur < Ymin1) Ycur = Ymin1;
          cur(); prnum(240, Ycur); break; /* Up    */
        case 80:
          cur(); Ycur += stsize;
          if (Ycur > Ymax1) Ycur = Ymax1;
          cur(); prnum(240, Ycur); break; /* Down  */
        default: message("Invalid");
      }
    } else
    if (ch == '>')
    { stsize *= 2;
      if (stsize > 200) stsize = 200; /* Maximum step size = 200 */
      prnum(80, stsize);
    } else
```

```
    if (ch == '<')
    { stsize /= 2;
      if (stsize == 0) stsize = 1;
      prnum(80, stsize);
    } else message("Invalid");
  }
  to_text();
}

window()
{ Xmin1 = 4; Xmax1 = X__max - 4; Ymin1 = 22; Ymax1 = Y__max - 14;
  imove(Xmin1, Ymin1); idraw(Xmax1, Ymin1); idraw(Xmax1, Ymax1);
  idraw(Xmin1, Ymax1); idraw(Xmin1, Ymin1);
  textXY(8, 0, "Use the four arrow keys to move the cursor.");
  imove(8, 11);
  text("Use > to increase, or < to decrease the stepsize.");
  text("    Press Q to quit.");
  Ybottext = Ymax1 +3; textXY(8, Ybottext, "Stepsize:");
  textXY(128, Ybottext, "X =");
  textXY(208, Ybottext, "Y =");
}

cur()
{ int i, j, dm;
  dm=drawmode; drawmode=0; /* change color, using xor */
  for (j=-2; j<=2; j+=4)
  for (i=-4; i<=4; i++) dot(Xcur+i, Ycur+j);
  dot(Xcur-4, Ycur-1); dot(Xcur-3, Ycur-1);
  dot(Xcur+3, Ycur-1); dot(Xcur+4, Ycur-1);
  dot(Xcur-4, Ycur); dot(Xcur-3, Ycur); dot(Xcur+3, Ycur);
  dot(Xcur+4, Ycur);   dot(Xcur, Ycur);
  dot(Xcur-4, Ycur+1); dot(Xcur-3, Ycur+1);
  dot(Xcur+3, Ycur+1); dot(Xcur+4, Ycur+1);
  drawmode=dm;

}

prnum(X, num) int X, num;
{ char str[4];
  sprintf(str, "%3d", num); textXY(X, Ybottext, str);
}

message(str) char *str;
{ textXY(Xmax1 - 64, Ybottext, str);
}
```

The heart of the main program is a loop in which one or two characters are read and processed each time. The external variables $X\_\_max$, $Y\_\_max$, $drawmode$ are defined in the module GRPACK (discussed in the previous chapters), and so are the functions $initgr$, to_text, $imove$, $idraw$, $text$, $textXY$. The program is not exactly practical, but it shows the basic elements of interactive graphics more clearly than a more complex program would have done. Figure 6.2 shows the screen at the beginning of program execution. Since the current cursor position was obtained by the statements

```
Xcur = Xmin1; Ycur = Ymin1;
```

the cursor is at the top-left corner of the window. If we move it downwards, the top window boundary will appear as a full line segment, not damaged by the previous position of the cursor.

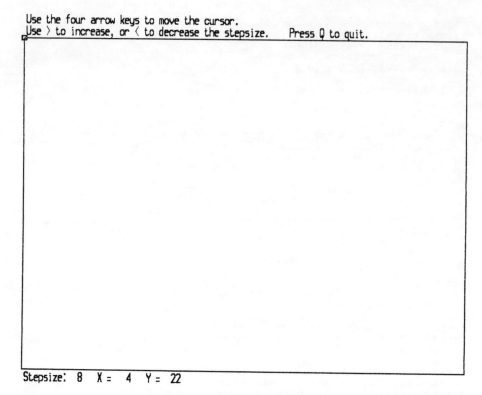

Fig. 6.2. Initial cursor position

6.3 SKETCH OPERATIONS

We shall now extend program CURSOR.C, and provide a convenient means to draw and erase horizontal and vertical line segments. Interactively inserting and erasing lines of text is another subject we shall deal with in this section. We shall move the cursor in the same way as in the previous section, but it will be possible to leave its trail on the screen. We regard the cursor as a pen, with its point either on or above a sheet of paper. For these two pen positions, we shall use the commands:

    PD: Pen Down
    PU: Pen Up

Obviously, a moving pen does not write anything if it is up. If it is down, however, things are much more interesting. Unlike an ordinary pen, our imaginary pen can also be used to erase what was written previously. We shall use the same three 'drawing modes' as in Section 3.1, with associated commands:

    PP: Pen Positive (drawing mode = 1)
    PN: Pen Negative (drawing mode = −1)
    PA: Pen Alternate (drawing mode = 0)

Recall that with drawing mode 0 the pen alternately writes and erases, hence the chosen command name. Altogether, we have $2 \times 3 = 6$ states for the pen, since the last three commands are independent from the pen position commands PD and PU. However, the pen is disabled if it is up, so we have only four interesting cases:

PU, (PD, PP), (PD, PN), (PD, PA)

We sometimes do not remember which commands we have given, so it will be helpful if we display the pen position and the drawing mode in the left-hand margin of the screen, outside the window. For the drawing mode, we shall use the letters P, N, A, which stand for 'positive', 'negative' and 'alternate', respectively. The function *dmode* takes care of this.

```
dmode(m) int m; /*  1 = Positive,  -1 = Negative,  0 = Alternate  */
{ textXY(0, 55, m == 1 ? "P" : m == -1 ? "N" : "A");
  drawmode = m;
}
```

We could have dealt with the pen position in the same way, displaying 'D' for Down and 'U' for Up. However, it is nice to use pictures instead, as shown in Fig. 6.3.

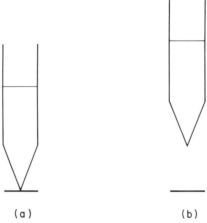

(a)   (b)

Fig. 6.3. Pen position: (a) Down, (b) Up

This picture of the pen position will also appear in the left-hand margin of the screen. This picture can easily be produced by displaying the letter H on top of the letter V, along with a horizontal line segment below the V, as written by the following function:

```
penposition(p) int p; /* 1 = down,  0 = up */
{ int dm;
  dm=drawmode; drawmode=1;
  textXY(0, p ? 27 : 40, "  ");  /* clear old pen portion */
  textXY(0, p ? 32 : 27, "H");
  textXY(0, p ? 40 : 35, "V");   /* a picture of a pen */
  draw_line(0, 48, 6, 48);       /* the paper on which the pen writes */
  pendown=p; drawmode=dm;
}
```

The best way to see how all this works is to use it yourself. After starting program execution, it may be desirable to alter the stepsize (pressing '>' or '<'), so that a reasonable number of steps are needed for each line segment we are drawing. The larger the stepsize, the easier it is to draw several line segments of exactly the same length and to return exactly in an endpoint of some line segment drawn previously. (For the latter, we shall use a more powerful method in Section 6.4.) Especially if we are frequently erasing portions of line segments immediately after drawing them, the 'alternate' line-drawing mode is to be recommended. There is a little programming problem associated with this. Recall that in the function *draw_line* we have inserted an extra call of the function *dot* to prevent the occurrence of little holes in line segments drawn with *drawmode* = 0, as discussed in Section 3.1. Now suppose that in this mode we draw line segment AB, and immediately after this we erase it by 'drawing' line segment BA. Then for point B the function *dot* is called three times, due to the extra call just mentioned, so that point will not vanish as it ought to. To solve this problem, we shall compare the direction of each line segment that is drawn with the direction of the previous line segment, and if it is opposite, we shall call *dot* for the fourth time in the point (B) where the direction reverses. Each time the cursor moves a step, we store the coordinates *Xcur* and *Ycur* of the point it is leaving in the variables *Xold* and *Yold*. After updating either *Xcur* or *Ycur* as a consequence of the move, the main task of function *lseg*, if the pen is down, is to perform the call

```
draw_line(Xold, Yold, Xcur, Ycur)
```

In addition to this, it examines the directions, and calls *dot* if necessary, depending on the directions of the new and the old line segments. Program SKETCH.C differs from its predecessor CURSOR.C of Section 6.2 both in that the functions *lseg*, *penposition* and *dmode* have been added, and in some modifications of the main program.

```
/* SKETCH.C: A demonstration program for sketch operations */

extern int X__max, Y__max, drawmode;
int Xmin1, Xmax1, Ymin1, Ymax1, Ybottext, Xcur, Ycur, stsize=8,
    pendown, Xold, Yold;

main()
{ char ch;
  initgr();
  window();
  dmode(1);          /* drawmode = 1 */
  penposition(0);    /* pendown = 0  */
  prnum(80, stsize);
  Xcur = Xmin1; Ycur = Ymin1; cur();
  prnum(160, Xcur); prnum(240, Ycur);
  while (ch = getch(), ch = toupper(ch), ch != 'Q')
  { message("        "); /* Clear message area */
    if (ch == 0)   /* This happens if an arrow key is pressed */
    { ch = getch(); Xold = Xcur; Yold = Ycur;
      switch (ch)
      { case 75:
          cur(); Xcur -= stsize;
          if (Xcur < Xmin1) Xcur = Xmin1;
          lseg(); cur(); prnum(160, Xcur); break; /* Left  */
        case 77:
          cur(); Xcur += stsize;
          if (Xcur > Xmax1) Xcur = Xmax1;
          lseg(); cur(); prnum(160, Xcur); break; /* Right */
```

```
      case 72:
        cur(); Ycur -= stsize;
        if (Ycur < Yminl) Ycur = Yminl;
        lseg(); cur(); prnum(240, Ycur); break; /* Up     */
      case 80:
        cur(); Ycur += stsize;
        if (Ycur > Ymaxl) Ycur = Ymaxl;
        lseg(); cur(); prnum(240, Ycur); break; /* Down  */
      default: message("Invalid");
    }
  } else
  if (ch == '>')
  { stsize *= 2;
    if (stsize > 200) stsize = 200; /* Maximum step size = 200 */
    prnum(80, stsize);
  } else
  if (ch == '<')
  { stsize /= 2;
    if (stsize == 0) stsize = 1;
    prnum(80, stsize);
  } else
  if (ch == 'P')
  { ch = getch(); ch = toupper(ch);
    switch (ch)
    { case 'D': penposition(1); break;
      case 'U': penposition(0); break;
      case 'P': dmode(1); break;
      case 'N': dmode(-1); break;
      case 'A': dmode(0); brcak;
      default: message("P ???");
    }
  } else message("Invalid");
  }
  to_text();
}
window()
{ Xminl = 12; Xmaxl = X__max - 4; Yminl = 22; Ymaxl = Y__max - 14;
  imove(Xminl, Yminl); idraw(Xmaxl, Yminl); idraw(Xmaxl, Ymaxl);
  idraw(Xminl, Ymaxl); idraw(Xminl, Yminl);
  textXY(8, 0, "Use the four arrow keys to move the cursor.");
  imove(8, 11);
  text("Use > to increase, or < to decrease the stepsize.");
  text("    Press Q to quit.");
  Ybottext = Ymaxl +3; textXY(8, Ybottext, "Stepsize:");
  textXY(128, Ybottext, "X =");
  textXY(208, Ybottext, "Y =");
}
cur()
{ int i, j, dm;
  dm=drawmode; drawmode=0; /* change color, using xor */
  for (j=-2; j<=2; j+=4)
  for (i=-4; i<=4; i++) dot(Xcur+i, Ycur+j);
  dot(Xcur-4, Ycur-1); dot(Xcur-3, Ycur-1);
  dot(Xcur+3, Ycur-1); dot(Xcur+4, Ycur-1);
  dot(Xcur-4, Ycur); dot(Xcur-3, Ycur); dot(Xcur+3, Ycur);
  dot(Xcur+4, Ycur);   dot(Xcur, Ycur);
  dot(Xcur-4, Ycur+1); dot(Xcur-3, Ycur+1);
  dot(Xcur+3, Ycur+1); dot(Xcur+4, Ycur+1);
  drawmode=dm;
}
prnum(X, num) int X, num;
{ char str[4];
  sprintf(str, "%3d", num); textXY(X, Ybottext, str);
}
```

```
message(str) char *str;
{ textXY(Xmax1 - 64, Ybottext, str);
}


lseg()
/* If pendown, draw line segment from (Xold, Yold) to (Xcur, Ycur) */
{ static int prevdown,
        /* Was previously a line segment drawn to old point? */
    prevdirection, direction;
  if (pendown)
  { draw_line(Xold, Yold, Xcur, Ycur);
    direction = Xcur < Xold ? -1 :
                Xcur > Xold ?  1 :
                Ycur < Yold ? -2 :
                Ycur > Yold ?  2 : 0;
    /* If prevdirection + direction == 0, and drawmode == 0, a line
       segment just drawn is erased; beware of an extra call of dot
       in the point of reversal, performed in  draw_line. */
    if (prevdown && drawmode==0 && prevdirection + direction == 0)
      dot(Xold, Yold); /* fourth call of dot in (Xold, Yold) */
  }
  prevdown = pendown; prevdirection = direction;
}


penposition(p) int p; /* 1 = down,   0 = up */
{ int dm;
  dm=drawmode; drawmode=1;
  textXY(0, p ? 27 : 40, "  ");   /* clear old pen portion */
  textXY(0, p ? 32 : 27, "H");
  textXY(0, p ? 40 : 35, "V");   /* a picture of a pen */
  draw_line(0, 48, 6, 48);    /* the paper on which the pen writes */
  pendown=p; drawmode=dm;
}


dmode(m) int m; /*  1 = Positive,  -1 = Negative,  0 = Alternate  */
{ textXY(0, 55, m == 1 ? "P" : m == -1 ? "N" : "A");
  drawmode = m;
}
```

6.4 DIG USER'S GUIDE

A great many facilities of our CAD program still have to be developed, and it would be awkward if we should discuss a long series of programs each being an extension of its predecessor; CURSOR.C and SKETCH.C would be the first two programs of such a series. Although such a bottom-up approach actually has led to our final CAD program, top-down program development is usually preferred in the presentation of software. So from now on we shall discuss our complete end product, DIG, first in the terminology of the user and only after that we shall have a look at the program text. The rest of this section is meant as a user's guide for DIG. Some aspects already dealt with in previous sections will be briefly repeated here, so that this user's guide will be independent of the rest of the book.

It is a good idea to use the commands under consideration in practice when you are studying them, so unless your ambitions are purely theoretical, I advise you to buy the program disk with the DIG program from the publisher (John Wiley & Sons).

6.4.1 Program start and end; workstates

We can start program execution in two ways, namely by typing either

DIG

or

DIG −P

(Small letters may be used instead of capital letters.)

The option −P should be used if you have a matrix printer (connected with the parallel printer port) and you wish to produce a hard copy of the graphics results displayed on the screen. The effect of this option is that on the printer horizontal and vertical dimensions tally, in other words, that circles are printed as circles, and squares as squares. This is achieved by adapting those dimensions when the picture appears on the screen so that they will be printed correctly. The price to be paid for this is that on the screen the dimensions will not tally, so with the option −P circles are displayed on the screen as ellipses. The opposite applies if the option −P is omitted. In that case, circles appear as circles on the screen, but as ellipses on the printer. Note that you can print (with the commands P0, P1, P2, discussed below), even if you have not used the option −P; only the dimensions will then be different.

After starting the program, we are asked to enter a file name. The picture that we are going to produce will eventually be written onto this file, so be cautious not to use the name of an existing file with valuable data! The best way to prevent this is to use a file-name extension, say, .PIC for picture files. Having typed the file name, say,

DRAWING.PIC,

a small menu of commands is displayed. We now either type H, for help, or switch to one of the two graphics 'workstates' called 'line-drawing' or 'alpha'. The commands to achieve this are WL and WA, respectively. The alpha workstate is needed if we wish text to appear in the picture. Let us assume that we want to draw lines in a picture first, so we type:

WL

This command changes the entire screen. A window appears, with some text in the top and bottom margin, as shown in Fig. 6.4.

As shown in the top margin, we can return to text mode by typing WT. After this, we can use the command Q to quit the program. The picture is then written to the file with the name given at the start of the program. If the picture is not worth saving, we can simply use Ctrl C instead of Q.

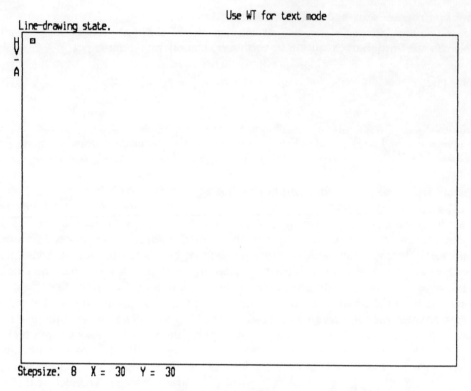

Fig. 6.4. Initial screen

6.4.2 Cursor, pen position and drawing modes

Normally, before we use the commands WT and Q, we want to draw a picture. This can be done in several ways. Near the top-left corner of the window there is a small square, which is called the *cursor*. It can be moved by pressing the four arrow keys located at the right-hand part of the keyboard. The default step size of cursor movements is eight pixels. We can increase or decrease it by by pressing '>' or '<', respectively. Notice that the current step size is displayed in the bottom margin of the screen. If we now press the key with the arrow pointing to the right, the cursor moves one step to the right, and so on. The left-hand margin of the screen shows a little picture of a pen with its point a little higher than a sheet of paper represented by a small horizontal line. With this pen position, any cursor movements will not draw anything. This will be different after we have entered the command

PD

which means 'Pen Down'. This command lowers the pen somewhat, so that its point touches the paper, as shown in the left-hand margin. If we now move the cursor, the pen draws a line like a normal pen. We can lift the pen by using the command

PU

which means Pen Up, and lower it somewhere else, and so on. Unlike an ordinary pen, this imaginary pen can also erase lines that have been drawn previously. Just below the pen picture in the left-hand margin, the letter A is shown, which means 'Alternate'. This is one of the three possible 'drawing modes', the two others being 'Positive' (P), and 'Negative' (N). The corresponding commands PA, PP, PN causes a transition to the drawing mode given by the second letter of these commands. After PP, the pen can only write, like an ordinary pen. The opposite holds after PN, that is, the pen can then only erase. So in the negative drawing mode, cursor movements will darken all pixels encountered. The 'alternate' drawing mode will reverse the pixel state. On a dark screen it is similar to the positive drawing mode, but when we move the cursor to a pixel that is lit, it will turn dark. Like drawing, erasing can take place only if the pen is down. All this might seem confusing, but it really is not, thanks to the fact that both the current pen position (Up/Down) and the current drawing mode (P/N/A) are displayed in the left-hand margin. In the bottom line, not only the step size, but also the X- and Y-coordinates are shown in digital form. This enables us to note the exact position of the cursor so as to return to it later. However, we have a more powerful means for this as we shall see in 6.4.4, when we introduce the concept of 'marked points'. Let us use the term 'sketching' for the way of line drawing discussed so far. It is useful only for simple applications, since it does not even enable us to draw slanting lines. Before we deal with more interesting line-drawing possibilities, let's first discuss a very simple subject, namely the 'alpha workstate'.

6.4.3 The alpha workstate

As mentioned above, we enter the alpha workstate by the command WA. This is possible not only when we are in the 'text state', but also in the 'line-drawing state'. (The more usual term 'mode' instead of 'state' would be confusing, since we already use that term for the three 'drawing-modes' P, N, A.) In the alpha workstate, all characters that are entered appear on the screen at the position of the cursor. So pieces of text are inserted very easily, in the same way as with a ordinary screen editor (but we now have the possibility to choose any line distance we like!). We can also use the backspace key to correct typing errors. The cursor then moves somewhat to the left and the incorrect character is removed. The space key has a similar effect, but obviously it moves the cursor to the right. It is nice that we can use these two keys to erase not only pieces of text, but also portions of a picture! So if in line-drawing state we have drawn something which we don't like, we have another means to erase it, namely by using the command WA and combining cursor movements with the space and the backspace keys. Since any text entered in alpha state will only be copied to the screen, we need another means to leave this state. To this end we use the Ctrl key: instead of, for example WL, we first press the key Ctrl, and when this key is still down, we press W and then L. (When pressing L the Ctrl key need no longer be kept down). The top margin of the screen shows how to switch to the text workstate, with or without the Ctrl key. Instead, we can switch directly from the alpha state to the line-drawing state, and vice versa.

6.4.4 Slanting lines and sets of marked points

We shall now deal with lines that are not necessarily horizontal or vertical. For example, let us draw the triangle ABC, where A, B and C may be any three points inside the screen window, not lying on the same line. We then proceed as follows:

1. We move the cursor to point A and type SA.
2. We move the cursor to point B and type L.
3. We move the cursor to point C and type L.
4. We move the cursor near point A, and type first F and then L.
5. We type SI or SC.

   To understand what happens in these steps, we must know that a set (or collection) of marked points is used. Initially, this set is empty. Many commands have the effect that the current point is marked with a cross (×) and at the same time added to the set. The command SA does this and nothing else, but there are other commands that perform some other task besides. For example, the command L also marks the current point (and adds it to the set), but its main task is to draw a line segment between the previous marked point and the current point. The command F is used to find the nearest marked point, and to move the cursor to it. This enables us to move the cursor exactly to some marked point very quickly. In the example of triangle ABC, I assumed that initially the points A, B and C were not given as marked points. When we draw the side CA, however, point A is a marked point, so here we can benefit from the F command. Without it, we would have had some difficulty in locating the cursor exactly in point A. In the last step, we can choose between the commands SI (Set Invisible) and SC (Set Clear). Both commands cause the crosses to disappear from the screen, but do not confuse them: Although the marks disappear, the command SI does not alter the set, and the F command can still be used. So after this command we still have the same marked points as before, but the marks are made invisible. They can be made visible again by the same command. This will be clear if we know that SI internally uses the 'alternate' line-drawing mode, discussed in 6.4.1. So SI actually 'toggles' the marks from visible to invisible and vice versa. The command SC, on the other hand, clears the set of marked points, so after it there are no marked points and the command F won't work anymore. For the sake of completeness, there is also the command SD (Delete a single Set point). If we move the cursor to some marked point (preferably by using F!) and we type SD, that point is removed from the set, and its mark on the screen, if visible, disappears. The set can contain at most 4000 marked points.

6.4.5 Block commands

We sometimes wish to manipulate certain portions of a picture. A block is a rectangular region with horizontal and vertical sides, located inside the screen window. It is fully determined if its top-left and its bottom-right corners are given. We shall call these two points the begin and the end of the block. The current cursor position is used for either point when we use the following two commands:

    BB (Block begin: the current position is the top-left corner)
    BK (Block end: the current position is the bottom-right corner).

(As a side effect, these two points are marked and consequently added to the set of marked points.) The rectangle itself will be visible after the command BK is given. Do not worry about long horizontal and vertical lines that appear as a result of the command BB; as soon as BK is typed they will have their proper lengths. If you wish the rectangle to disappear (retaining the block definition), simply type BE (Block Erase). This command erases only the rectangle that is the boundary; the contents of the block remain unaffected. In contrast to this, the command BD (Block Delete) deletes the entire block, including its contents. We shall now see why blocks are useful. We can copy or move a block using the commands BC and BM, respectively. These commands use the current cursor position as the begin (that is, the top-left corner) of the new block we are creating. With BC, the block is copied, so the original block remains unaffected. This is not the case with BM, which really moves the block, deleting the old one. Note that at most one block can exist at a time, so if a block has been defined, there is no problem about which block is meant in a command. Two other very important commands are BW (Block Write) and BR (Block Read). They ask for the name of a file in the top margin of the screen. The command BW then writes the block to that file, and the command BR reads a block from the file and places it on the screen such that the current cursor position will be the begin of the block. As in 6.4.1, a warning may not be superfluous with respect of the file name, since if an existing file is used its old contents will be destroyed by the command BW. Again, it is a good idea to use an extension, such as .SYM in such file names. Such a file may contain some symbol that we often need. Instead of drawing the symbol each time we need it, we can simply 'load' it from its file and insert it wherever we wish. It is not without reason that here I propose an extension (.SYM) different from the one (.PIC) for the entire picture (see 6.4.1). These two types of files are incompatible with respect to their data format, so they must not be confused.

6.4.6 Vectors, circles and arcs

In mathematics vectors are normally represented as arrows. Before discussing the way our vectors are used, let's see how we can define one. If we type I, the cursor position will be the initial point of the vector, and in a similar way the command E defines its endpoint. Thus the vector is directed from I to E. Point I is marked by a cross ($+$), different from the cross ($\times$) that marks set points. After typing E, an arrow appears, with the arrow point in E. A full circle with center I and radius IE is drawn by the command CF, provided that the circle fits into the screen boundaries. If not, an error message appears. If in that case we want the circle to be drawn as far as the screen boundaries permit, we should not use CF, but C^+ (or $C-$), see below, with an angle of 360°. (If we know that there are no such problems, we had better use CF, however, for with this command the circle is drawn much faster than with $C+$ or $C-$.) We normally wish the arrow IE to disappear when we do not need it anymore. This will happen when a new point is defined as an initial point I. The commands I and E have the side effect that the defined points I and E are also added to the set, and consequently marked x as well. (As we have seen in 6.4.4, we can get rid of these marks by the commands SI, SD, and SC). If not a full circle but only some part of it (an arc) is desired, we can use the commands $C+$ and $C-$.

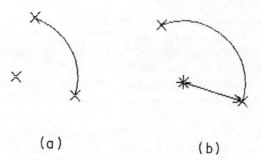

(a)   (b)

Fig. 6.5. Arc, (a) with a given angle, and (b) with an endpoint on a given line

Again, the center will be the initial point I of the vector that we have defined previously. The arc will start at the endpoint E of the vector, and be drawn counter-clockwise if C+ or clockwise if C− has been given. However, we still have to specify something about the endpoint of the arc. If the cursor is still in the end point E of the vector when we give the command C+ or C−, we are requested to enter the angle (in degrees) between the lines IE and IP, where P is the endpoint of the arc. The arc in Fig. 6.5a was drawn in this way, using C+ and an angle of 90°.

Initially, there was an arrow IE similar to the one that is still visible in Fig. 6.5b, so the arc was drawn in the upward direction. If we give the command C+ or C− while the cursor does no longer coincide with point E, we are not asked to enter an angle, but instead, the endpoint of the arc will lie on the line through point I and the current position of the cursor. This method was used in Fig. 6.5b; it is useful when we know a line on which the endpoint of the arc should lie rather than the angle of the arc expressed in degrees. Note that in Fig. 6.5a the arrow and the special mark (+) of point I have disappeared. This happened when the new point I, that is, the center of Fig. 6.5b was defined. The latter point I still shows that mark, together with the mark (×) used for set points. These two marks (and all others as well) can be made to disappear, as we have discussed.

There are some additional commands that deal with vectors. They consist of two letters, the first of which is V:

VS: Replace the vector with a normal (drawn) line segment.
VD: Replace the vector with a dashed line segment.
VL: Replace the vector with a long line through I and E. The line will be as long as the window permits.
VK: Keep the arrow. After this command, the arrow will not disappear when the command I is given to define a new initial point I. However, after the latter command, the old vector is no longer available if, for example, a circle is to be drawn.
VA: Make the arrow point of the vector invisible if it is visible and vice versa. On the screen, the effect of this command seems the same as that of VS. However, after VS the vector is no longer available, but after VA it is.

We say that the command VA toggles the arrow point. The following commands also turn visible objects invisible, and vice versa:

+: Toggle the mark (+) that is used for an initial vector point I.

✱: Toggle the cursor itself.

·: Toggle the very point denoted by the cursor.

6.4.7 Constructing a new point

We can define a direction, and use it subsequently to construct a new point. Since directions are essential in the following three commands, they begin with the letter D:

DD: Define a direction.

DU: Define a unit of length, to be used in connection with the former command.

DN: Construct a new point.

After typing DD, we are asked to enter either an angle (in degrees) or an asterisk (✱). If we enter an angle, it defines the final direction of an imaginary arrow, originally pointing horizontally to the right, and rotated through that angle counter-clockwise. If instead of an angle we type an asterisk, we must have defined a vector (see 6.4.6) previously, and the direction of that vector is then used. Remember that after typing an asterisk or the value of some angle, we have to press the Enter key (also called Return key). If we have been using the asterisk, the direction of the vector that existed at that time will be remembered, even if we define a new vector afterwards. This is rather important in connection with command DU and DN, as we will see. The command DU enables us to define a new unit of length, which by default was defined as one inch. Before typing DU, we have to set up a vector IE. After typing DU, the following question is displayed:

How many units?

If we type 1, the length of the vector will be used as the new unit. We may also type an integer greater than 1, say, n. Then the unit of length will be such that the vector has length n. If we now place the cursor somewhere, say in point P, and we type DN, we are asked to enter either a length or an asterisk. The length is to be expressed in the defined unit; it may be any real number. The new point, say Q, is then constructed such that PQ has that length and the direction defined previously by DD. This will work only if Q lies within the screen window. An error message will appear if that is not the case. As with DD, after DN we may enter an asterisk (followed by pressing the Enter key). In this case the newly constructed point Q will lie on the (imaginary) line through the initial point I and the endpoint E of the current vector. Thus, when using this facility, we should have defined the vector somewhere on the line we want point Q to lie on.

An important application of these commands is dividing a given line segment AB into some (let us say, *n*) line segments all of the same length. To this end, we define a vector whose initial point is A and whose endpoint is B; we then type DU, and after the question 'How many units?' is displayed, we type the value of *n*. We also type DD followed by an asterisk to define the correct direction. Then we move the cursor to point A (with the help of the command F), and we type DN. The question 'Length or *:' is then answered 1, and the first desired point is constructed. We then type DN, followed by 1, again, and so on, and all desired points appear where they belong. Since all new points are marked (×) and added to the set, we can return to them easily whenever we want, each time using the F command.

Besides dividing a line segment by n, we can also extend it, such that the new line segment will be n times as long as the original one. Again, we apply the command DU to the given line segment AB (after promoting it to a vector with the commands I and E), but now we give it length 1. With the cursor in A, we then type DN followed by the value n, which yields the desired point.

6.4.8 Using a matrix printer; area filling

We will now discuss four commands typed as two characters, the first of which is P. If a matrix printer is available, we can print the graphics results produced so far. Of course, any marks (×) denoting set points should be made invisible first (using SI, or SC), since they ought not to appear in our printed output. Also, any mark (+) denoting an initial point of a vector should be erased with the command +, see 6.4.6. Before typing a print command, we must check if the printer is switched on. Distances in the horizontal and the vertical directions will tally only if we have used the option −P when we started DIG, see 6.4.1. If not, circles on the screen will be printed as ellipses. A print command consists of the letter P, followed by one of the number 0, 1, 2. Remember, the higher the number, the larger the drawing:

> P0: Print everything that is inside the window; the window itself is not printed.
> P1: Print everything inside the window, including the window itself, but not the text in the margins.
> P2: Print the entire screen, including the text in the margins.

We conclude this section with a command that has nothing to do with printing, except its first letter. Starting at the current cursor position, the command

> PF

fills an entire closed region with pixels that are lit. The boundary of that region may be composed of any line segments and arcs. If there are holes in the region (which are smaller regions in which the cursor does not lie), these will not be filled. There is one extremely important point here, namely that the region should really be closed. For example, if in a polygon a single pixel on the boundary is missing, we may not notice this, and the smallest closed region will be much larger than we assume it to be. In that case, the horrible effect will be that many more pixels will be lit than we expect, usually to such an extent that the whole picture is destroyed. This effect is called 'bleeding'. It may be a good idea to save the entire picture first, which is done at the end of program execution. So we can stop the program, make a copy of the picture file, typing, for example

> COPY DRAWING.PIC DRAWING.BAK,

and start the program for the second time with the original file. Should then the command PF lead to bleeding, then we still have the back-up file DRAWING.BAK.

6.4.9 B-spline curve fitting

Not all drawings consist exclusively of straight lines and (parts of) circles. A well-known technique to construct a curve passing approximately through a number of given points is B-spline curve fitting. It yields extremely smooth curves, or, more precisely, curves with continuous second derivatives. I refer to my book *Programming Principles in Computer Graphics* for some more information about this method. Here we shall simply use it, and not deal with the underlying mathematics. In general, the curve constructed with B-splines will not pass exactly through the given points. We shall distinguish between open and closed curves. Let us assume that we have specified a sequence of $n + 1$ points $P_0, P_1, \ldots, P_n$, where n is not less than 3. We shall see shortly how this is done. Then we have two curve fitting commands, each consisting of two letters:

SF: Use the given $n + 1$ points to draw (or erase) a curve passing approximately through the $n - 1$ points $P_1, P_2, \ldots, P_{n-1}$ (F = Fitting)

SR: Use the given $n + 1$ points to draw (or erase) a closed curve passing approximately through all these points. (R = Round)

Since the alternating drawing mode is used, we can alternately draw and erase curves.

In 6.4.4 we discussed a set of marked points. This set will now be regarded as a point sequence, that is, the order of the points will matter. Although we deal with the same subject as in 6.4.4, we can no longer call it a set, since in a set the elements are unordered by definition. In a sequence, however, the order of the elements is significant. For example, $\{P_1, P_2, P_3\}$ and $\{P_2, P_3, P_1\}$ denote the same set, but they are different sequences. So we now use the term 'sequence' for what we used to call a set.

The command SA, and some other commands, such as I, normally extend the sequence at the end. We can move the cursor from one point in the sequence to another, using the following four commands (each consisting of two characters):

S<: Move the cursor to the initial point (P_0) of the sequence.

S>: Move the cursor to the final point (P_n) of the sequence.

S]: Move the cursor to the next point (if there is one).

S[: Move the cursor to the previous point (if there is one).

If we have used these commands or the command F (Find) to move the cursor to some point in the sequence, say, P_i, and subsequently move the cursor to somewhere else, say, Q, then the command SA will insert the new point Q immediately after P_i. So any points that followed P_i are shifted one position to the right. Analogously, the command SD, discussed in 6.4.4, deletes a point of the sequence, in such a way, that any following points are shifted one position to the left. So we now have some tools to update the sequence of marked points, taking the order of the elements into consideration.

Often we wish not the entire sequence but only some subsequence of it to be used for curve fitting. This can be done by establishing the vector IE between the initial point I and the endpoint E of the subsequence. If I is point P_i and E is point P_j, and we have

$$i \geqq 0$$
$$j - i > 2$$
$$j \leqq n$$

then the points P_k, where $k < i$ or $k > j$, are ignored.

  After we have constructed the curve, we usually want to see it on the screen without all the marks ($\times$). We then simply use the command SI, see 6.4.4. Beware of using SC too soon, since then the marked points are lost, whereas with SI they will reappear after the same command is given again.

6.4.10 Command summary

Here is a summary of Section 6.4, which might be handy as a quick reference:

Main command menu, shown at program start
....

WL   : Switch to line-drawing workstate.
WA   : Switch to graphics alpha workstate.
Q   : Quit; graphics results will be saved.
Ctrl C : Quit immediately.
H   : Help.

When H is pressed, the following secondary menu appears:
Press:
1   for program start and state switching
2   for cursor commands, pen position and drawing modes
3   for the alpha workstate
4   for commands to manipulate a set of marked points
5   for block commands
6   for vectors, circles and arcs
7   for directions, units of length, new points
8   for matrix printer usage and for area filling
9   for B-spline curve fitting
M   to return to the main menu
By pressing one of the keys $0, 1, \ldots, 9$, the corresponding paragraph appears, as shown below. After that, you may enter another digit to display a group of commands, or press M or H to display the main or help menu once again.

(1) Program start and state switching
....

DIG   : Start the program; dimensions are based on the screen.
DIG $-$P : Start the program; dimensions are based on the matrix printer.

Angles will have their proper sizes and circles will appear as circles on the printer if the option −P is used. If proper dimensions on the screen are more important than those on the printer, the option −P should not be used.

WL : Switch to line-drawing state.
WA : Switch to graphics alpha state.
WT : Switch to text state, to quit, or to ask for help.

Note: In graphics alpha state the Control key must be kept down when the letter W is entered for state switching.

(2) Cursor commands, pen position and drawing modes
....

The cursor is moved by pressing the arrow keys.
The step size is increased or decreased by pressing > or <.

PU : Pen Up.
PD : Pen Down.
PP : Pen in Positive drawing mode: use pen, when down, to draw.
PN : Pen in Negative drawing mode: use pen, when down, to rub out.
PA : Pen in Alternate drawing mode: use pen, when down, to 'toggle'.

The following commands may have confusing effects, so be cautious when using them:

✷ : Toggle cursor.
· : Toggle dot.
+ : Toggle O-cursor.

(3) The alpha workstate
....

Text appears in the drawing as it is entered. The backspace key may be used for corrections. Keep the Ctrl key down when pressing the first letter W of the state switching commands WT, WL.

(4) Commands to manipulate a set of marked points
....

All points in the set are marked X.

SA : Add point to set.
SD : Delete point from set.
SC : Clear the set.
SI : Toggle points in set (invisible/visible).
F   : Find the nearest point in the set, and move cursor to it.
L   : Use the point most recently added to the set as the 'old' point. Then a line segment is drawn from the old point to the current cursor position. Besides SA, the commands L and I also add points to the set.

See also (9).

(5) Block commands

....

BB : Begin of block, top-left corner.
BK : End of block, bottom-right corner.
BE : Erase (or draw again) block boundary.
BD : Delete the entire block.
BC : Block Copy.
BM : Block Move.
BW : Block Write.
BR : Block Read.

(6) Vectors, circles and arcs

....

I   : Define initial point I of vector.
E   : Define endpoint E of vector.
VA : Toggle arrow of vector (invisible/visible).
VS : Replace vector with line segment.
VD : Replace vector with dashed line segment.
VL : Replace vector with long line.
VK : Keep vector: the arrow is to be permanent.

With CF, C+, C−, point point I is the center and IE the radius.

CF : Draw a full circle.
C+ : Draw arc with a given angle, counter-clockwise.
C− : Similarly, clockwise.
      With C+ and C−, if the cursor is not in E, its position will be used to
      determine the angle of the arc.

(7) Directions, units of length, new points

....

The following three commands ask for a number or an asterisk. Don't forget to
press the Enter key after typing that number or asterisk.

DU : When this command is used, a vector IE must have been defined. The
      question 'How many units?' is displayed. If you now enter some integer value
      n, the unit of length is defined such that the length of IE is n, expressed in
      this unit. The unit may be used by subsequent DN commands.
DD : An angle measured from the positive X-axis is requested to define a
      direction. This direction will be used by subsequent DN commands. An
      asterisk means: use the direction of vector IE for this purpose.
DN : Find a new point in the current direction, at a given distance from the current
      cursor position. An asterisk means: place the point on the line IE.

(8) Output on a matrix printer; area filling

....

P0 : Print everything inside the window boundaries (not the boundaries
      themselves).

P1 : Print everything inside the boundaries, including the boundaries themselves.
P2 : Print the complete screen.
PF : Fill the closed region in which the cursor is lying. Beware of 'bleeding', which will happen if the region is not completely closed. Before giving the command PF, temporarily erase any marks, using SI.

(9) B-spline curve fitting
....

The set of marked points is now regarded as a sequence.

S< : Move the cursor to the initial point of the sequence.
S> : Move the cursor to the final point of the sequence.
S[: Move the cursor to the predecessor of the current marked point.
S] : Move the cursor to the successor of the current marked point.
SF : Draw (or erase) a curve that approximately passes through the marked points, with the exception of the initial and the final point.
SR : As SF,but now going round, drawing a closed curve.

If I and E coincide with appropriate points of the sequence, the subsequence beginning in I and ending in E is used instead of the entire sequence of marked points. (IE will be shown as an arrow.)

The sequence can be updated using SD and SA (see 4.). After moving the cursor to a marked point (using F, S], or S[), you can insert a new point immediately after that marked point by moving the cursor to the new point and using SA.

6.5 SOURCE TEXT

The program text for DIG consists of four modules, namely:

> DIG.C: the main program, listed in 6.5.1,
> DIGFUN.C: a large set of functions, listed in 6.5.2,
> DIGH.C: a function to print messages for help, listed in 6.5.3,
> GRPACK.C: a package of general graphics functions, listed in Section 4.5.

6.5.1 Program text of DIG.C (main program)

```
/* DIG.C: Drawing with Interactive Graphics      */
/*        (L. Ammeraal/John Wiley & Sons)         */
/*        This program uses functions defined in  */
/*        DIGFUN.C, DIGH.C, GRPACK.C.             */

extern int X__max, Y__max, drawmode, colorgr;

int Xminl, Xmaxl, Yminl, Ymaxl, Xcur, Ycur, stsize=8,
    pendown, Xold, Yold, keepvector,
    Xb=100, Yb=100, Xk=100, Yk=100;
char fil[30], workstate='T'; /* T = Textmode */

main(argc, argv) int argc; char **argv;
{ char ch, chl, str[2];
  int gr_entered=0, first=1, dm, pd;
  if (argc > 1)
  { if (argv[1][0] == '-' && toupper(argv[1][1]) == 'P')
    setprdim(); else         /* 'setprdim' is defined in GRPACK.C */
    { printf("Invalid program argument"); exit(1);
    }
  }
```

```
      printf("File name: "); scanf("%s", fil);
      while (1)
      { if (workstate == 'T')   /* WT: textmode (= initial state) */
        { if (first) { ch = 'M'; first = 0; } else ch = getche();
          ch = toupper(ch);
          if (ch == 'Q')
          { if (gr_entered && !colorgr)
            { printf(
"\nThe picture is now written to file %s; wait a moment, please.\n",
              fil);
              save();
            }
            exit(0);
          }
          if (ch=='H' || ch=='M') { menu(ch); continue; }
          if (ch=='W')
          { ch1=getche(); ch1 = toupper(ch1);   /* W = Workstate */
            if (ch1=='A' || ch1=='L')
                      /* WA: graphics alpha,  WL: line drawing and sketch */
            { wstate(ch1); gr_entered = 1; continue;
            }
          }
          menu('M'); continue;
        }

        /* We are now in one of the two graphics workstates WL and WA */
        ch=getch();
        if (ch == 0)   /* This happens if an arrow key is pressed */
        { ch = getch(); Xold = Xcur; Yold = Ycur;
          switch (ch)
          { case 75:
               cur(); Xcur -= stsize;
               if (Xcur < Xminl) Xcur = Xminl;
               lseg(); cur(); prnum(160, Xcur); break; /* Left  */
            case 77:
               cur(); Xcur += stsize;
               if (Xcur > Xmaxl) Xcur = Xmaxl;
               lseg(); cur(); prnum(160, Xcur); break; /* Right */
            case 72:
               cur(); Ycur -= stsize;
               if (Ycur < Yminl) Ycur = Yminl;
               lseg(); cur(); prnum(240, Ycur); break; /* Up     */
            case 80:
               cur(); Ycur += stsize;
          if (Ycur > Ymaxl) Ycur = Ymaxl;
          lseg(); cur(); prnum(240, Ycur); break; /* Down  */
          }
        continue;
      }
      message(" ");                 /* Clear the message area   */
      if (workstate=='A')           /* State WA: Graphics Alpha  */
      { if (ch == 23)               /* 23 == Ctrl W              */
        { ch1=getch(); ch1=toupper(ch1);
          if (ch1 < 32) ch1 += 64; /* Convert Ctrl-L into L etc. */
          if (ch1 == 'L' || ch1 == 'T' || ch1 == 'A')
          { wstate(ch1); continue;
          } else message("Ctrl-W ???");
        }
        if (ch == 13)    /* Return (or Enter) */
        { penposition(0) /* up */;
          cur(); /* Erase old cursor */
          Xcur = 10; Ycur += 15;
          if (Ycur > Ymaxl - 11) Ycur = Yminl + 1;
          cur(); /* Draw new cursor */
          continue;
        }
```

```
  cur();     /* delete old cursor */
  str[0]=(ch == 8 ? ' ' : ch); /* 8 = backspace */
  str[1]='\0';
  Xcur &= 0xFFF8; /* truncated to a multiple of 8 */
  if (ch == 8)
  { Xcur-=8; /* space to be written on position of last character */
    if (Xcur<Xminl) Xcur=Xminl;
  }
  textXY(Xcur, Ycur, str);
  Xcur += (ch == 8 ? 0 : 8);
  if (Xcur>Xmaxl) Xcur=Xmaxl;
  cur(); coord();
  continue;
}

/* We are now in state WL: Line drawing and sketching */
ch = toupper(ch);
if (ch == '>')
{ stsize *= 2;
  if (stsize > 200) stsize = 200; /* Maximum step size = 200 */
  prnum(80, stsize); continue;
}
if (ch == '<')
{ stsize /= 2;
  if (stsize == 0) stsize = 1;
  prnum(80, stsize); continue;
}
if (ch == 'P')
{ ch1 = getch(); ch1 = toupper(ch1);
  switch (ch1)
  { case 'D': penposition(1); break;
    case 'U': penposition(0); break;
    case 'P': dmode(1); break;
    case 'N': dmode(-1); break;
    case 'A': dmode(0); break;
    case '0': case '1': case '2':
            hardcopy(ch1); break;      /* output on matrix printer */
    case 'F': cur(); pixfill(Xcur, Ycur); cur(); break;
  }
  continue;
}

if (ch == 'W') /* workstate switching */
{ ch1=getch(); ch1=toupper(ch1);
  switch (ch1)
  { case 'A': case 'L': case 'T': wstate(ch1); break;
    default: message("W ???");
  }
  continue;
}
dm=drawmode; pd=pendown;
dmode(0); penposition(0);
if (ch=='B')
{ ch1=getch(); ch1=toupper(ch1);
  switch(ch1)
  {
  case 'B':                          /* block Begin  */
    Xb=Xcur; Yb=Ycur;
    if (Yb>Yminl) draw_line(Xb, Yb, Xmaxl, Yb);
    if (Xb>Xminl) draw_line(Xb, Yb, Xb, Ymaxl);
    addset(Xb, Yb);
    break;
  case 'K':                          /* blocK end */
    Xk=Xcur; Yk=Ycur;
    if (Xk<Xb || Yk<Yb) break;
    if (Yb>Yminl) draw_line(Xk, Yb, Xmaxl, Yb);
```

```
      if (Xb>Xmin1) draw_line(Xb, Yk, Xb, Ymax1);
      if (Xk<Xmax1) draw_line(Xk, Yb, Xk, Yk);
      if (Yk<Ymax1) draw_line(Xb, Yk, Xk, Yk);
      dot(Xb, Yb); dot(Xk, Yk); addset(Xk, Yk);
      break;
    case 'E':                              /* Erase rectangle */
      if (Yb>Ymin1) draw_line(Xb, Yb, Xk, Yb);
      if (Xk<Xmax1) draw_line(Xk, Yb, Xk, Yk);
      if (Yk<Ymax1) draw_line(Xk, Yk, Xb, Yk);
      if (Xb>Xmin1) draw_line(Xb, Yk, Xb, Yb);
      break;
    case 'C':                              /* Copy block   */
    case 'M': blcopy(ch1); break;          /* Move block   */
    case 'D': bldelete(); break;           /* Delete block */
    case 'W': blwrite(); break;            /* Write block  */
    case 'R': blread(); break;             /* Read block   */
    default: message("B ???");
    }
    continue;
}

if (ch=='D') /* define direction (DD) or unit of length (DU) */
{ ch1=getch(); ch1=toupper(ch1);
  switch (ch1)
  { case 'D': defdirection(); break;   /* direction   */
    case 'U': unit(); break;           /* unit length */
    case 'N': newpoint(); break;
    default: message("D ???");
  }
  continue;
}

if (ch=='C') /* Full circle (CF) or arc (C+, C-) */
{ ch1=getch(); ch1=toupper(ch1);
  switch (ch1)
  { case 'F': arc(0); break;
    case '+': arc(1); break;
    case '-': arc(-1); break;
    default: message("C ???");
  }
  continue;
}

if (ch=='S') /* Set and sequence manipulation */
{ ch1=getch(); ch1=toupper(ch1);
  switch (ch1)
  { case 'A': addset(Xcur, Ycur);
    break;                             /* Add P(Xcur, Ycur) to set */
    case 'C': clearset(); break;       /* Clear set                */
    case 'D': delpset(Xcur, Ycur);
    break;                             /* Remove P from list       */
    case 'I': inviset(); break;        /* Points of set invisible  */
    case '[': toseq(-1); break;        /* To previous sequence pnt */
    case ']': toseq(1); break;         /* To next sequence point   */
    case '<': toseq(-2); break;        /* To initial sequence point*/
    case '>': toseq(2); break;         /* To final sequence point  */
    case 'F': curvefit(0); break;      /* B-spline curve (open)    */
    case 'R': curvefit(1); break;      /* B-spline curve (closed)  */
    default: message("S ???");
  }
  continue;
}

if (ch=='F') { findset(); continue; }  /* find point in set */
if (ch=='I') { ipoint(); continue; }   /* initial point     */
if (ch=='L') { drawtoP(); continue; }  /* draw segment      */
if (ch=='E') { endpoint(); continue; }
```

```
    if (ch=='V')
    { chl=getch(); chl=toupper(chl);
      switch (chl)
      { case 'K': keepvector=1; break;
        case 'S': lsegment(0); break;     /* segment instead of arrow */
        case 'D': lsegment(1); break;     /* dashed segment          */
        case 'L': lsegment(2); break;     /* long line               */
        case 'A': arrow(); break;         /* erase/draw arrow        */
        default: message("V ???");
      }
      continue;
    }

    if (ch=='*') { cur(Xcur, Ycur); continue; }     /* toggle cursor   */
    if (ch=='.') { dot(Xcur, Ycur); continue; }     /* toggle dot      */
    if (ch=='+') { icursor(Xcur, Ycur); continue; }/* toggle I-cursor */
    dmode(dm); penposition(pd);
  }
}
```

6.5.2 Program text of DIGFUN.C (functions)

```
/* DIGFUN.C: Functions used in DIG.C, in alphabetical order. */
/*           See also DIGH.C and GRPACK.C.                    */
#include "stdio.h"
#include "math.h"
#define PI 3.14159265358979
#define PIDOUBLE 6.28318530717959
#define MAX 4000
extern int Xcur, Ycur, Xold, Yold, X__max, Y__max, colorgr,
  stsize, drawmode, Xmin1, Xmax1, Ymin1, Ymax1,
  Xb, Yb, Xk, Yk, keepvector, pendown;
extern float horfact, vertfact;
extern char workstate, fil[];

static int XY[2], Ybottext, displaymax,
    XI=-1, YI, XE, YE,
    vdefined, Xprev=-1, Yprev, XXold=-1, YYold,
    Xend1, Yend1, Xend2, Yend2, n, marksvisible=1;

static char str[80];
static float xxi, yyi, xxe, yye, xxl, yyl, dx, dy, r, phi0, phil,
            /* These variables obtain their values in 'geometrics'; */
            /*    they are used in 'arc', 'defdirection', 'lsegment' */
      xmin, xmax, ymin, ymax,
      un=1.0, phi=1000.0;

double fx(), fy();

struct SET { int XX, YY;} set[MAX+1];
      /* MAX+1 to accommodate sentinel */

addset(X1, Y1) int X1, Y1;    /* Add new point to set (SA) */
{ struct SET *p;
  int nn, n0, X0, Y0, i;
  if (n == MAX) { message("Set full"); return; }
  nn = find(X1, Y1);
  if (nn == n)
  { X0=Xprev; Y0=Yprev;
    if (X0 == X1 && Y0 == Y1) { X0=XXold; Y0=YYold; }
    n0 = find(X0, Y0);
    if (n0 == n) p = set+n; else
    { for (i=n-1; i>n0; i--) set[i+1]=set[i];
      p = set+n0+1;
    }
```

```
    p->XX = X1; p->YY = Y1; n++;
    if (marksvisible) mark(X1, Y1);
  }
  XXold=Xprev; YYold=Yprev;
  Xprev=X1; Yprev=Y1;
}

static double angle(xC, yC, x, y) double xC, yC, x, y;
{ /* angle between {(xC, yC), (x, y)} and positive x-axis */
  float alpha;
  if (fabs(x - xC) < .0005) return ((y > yC ? .5 : -.5) * PI);
  alpha = atan((y - yC)/(x - xC));
  return (x > xC ? alpha : alpha + PI);
}

arc(sign) int sign;    /* Draw arc (C+, C-) */
{ float delta, phi, phideg, phi_0, theta;
  int X, Y, n, i, Xold=-1, Yold=-1;

  /* Draw circle arc, centre I(XI, YI),
                  first point E(XE, YE),
     endpoint on CP, where P(Xcur, Ycur), or specified by angle phi.
     sign (sense of rotation): 1 = counter clockwise,  -1 = clockwise
     If sign = 0, a full circle is drawn.                         */

  if (!vdefined) { message("Vector?"); return; }
  geometrics(); phi_0=phi0; phi=phi1-phi0;
  if (sign == 0)
  { if (xxi-r < xmin || xxi+r > xmax || yyi-r < ymin || yyi+r > ymax)
    message("Outside screen"); else circle(xxi, yyi, r);
    return;
  }
  if (XE==Xcur && YE==Ycur)
  { if (enquire("Angle: ", str)==0) { invalid(); return; }
    sscanf(str, "%f", &phideg);
    phi = PI*phideg/180.0;
  }
  n = (int) (80.0 * r * phi);      /* 80 points per inch! */
  n = abs(n);
  delta = sign * phi/n;
  for (i=1; i<=n; i++)
  { theta = phi_0 + i * delta;
    X = IX(xxi+r*cos(theta)); Y = IY(yyi+r*sin(theta));
    if ((X != Xold || Y != Yold) &&
        (X > Xmin1 && X < Xmax1 && Y > Ymin1 && Y < Ymax1)) dot(X, Y);
    Xold=X; Yold=Y;
  }
  addset(Xold, Yold);
}

arrow()    /* Erase/draw arrow (VA) */
{ float a, b, xdif, ydif, tx, ty;
  a=dx/r; b=dy/r;
  xdif=xxe-0.125*a; ydif=yye-0.125*b;
  tx=0.05*b; ty=0.05*a;
  clipdraw(xdif+tx, ydif-ty, xxe, yye);
  clipdraw(xdif-tx, ydif+ty, xxe, yye);
}

blcopy(ch1) char ch1; /* Copy a block (BC, BM) */
{ int Blength, Bwidth, X, Y, XX1, YY1, invicalled=0;
  cur();
  if (marksvisible) { inviset(); invicalled=1; }
  if (ch1=='M') delpinblock();
    /* Remove all points inside old block from set */
```

```
  Blength=Xk-Xb; Bwidth=Yk-Yb;
  for (X=Xb; X<=Xk; X++)
  for (Y=Yb; Y<=Yk; Y++)
  if (pixlit(X, Y))
  { XX1=Xcur+X-Xb; YY1=Ycur+Y-Yb;
    if (XX1<=Xmaxl && YY1<=Ymaxl) dot(XX1, YY1);
    if (ch1=='M')
    { drawmode=-1; dot(X, Y); drawmode=0;
    }
  }
  Xb=Xcur; Yb=Ycur; Xk=Xcur+Blength; Yk=Ycur+Bwidth;
  if (Xk>Xmaxl) Xk=Xmaxl;
  if (Yk>Ymaxl) Yk=Ymaxl;
  cur();
  addset(Xb, Yb); addset(Xk, Yk);
  if (invicalled) inviset();
}

bldelete()     /* Delete a block (BD) */
{ int X, Y;
  delpinblock();
  drawmode=-1;   /* delete block */
  cur();
  for (X=Xb; X<=Xk; X++)
  for (Y=Yb; Y<=Yk; Y++) dot(X, Y);
  drawmode=0; cur();
}


blread()     /* Read a block (BR) */
{ FILE *fp; int Blength, Bwidth, j, X, Y, buflen;
  unsigned char bitbuf[100], *p;
  if (enquire("File: ", str)==0) return;
  fp=fopen(str, "rb");
  if (fp==NULL)
  { message("Unknown file"); return;
  }
  cur();
  fread((char *)&Blength, 1, sizeof(int), fp);
  fread((char *)&Bwidth, 1, sizeof(int), fp);
  Xb=Xcur; Yb=Ycur; Xk=Xb+Blength; Yk=Yb+Bwidth;
  buflen=(Blength>>3)+1;
  for (Y=Yb; Y<=Yk; Y++)
  { fread(bitbuf, 1, buflen, fp);
    j=0; p=bitbuf;
    if (Y<=Ymaxl)
    for (X=Xb; X<=Xk; X++)
    { if (*p & 0x80 && X<=Xmaxl) dot(X, Y);
      *p <<= 1;
      if (++j == 8) { p++; j=0; }
    }
  }
  if (Xk>Xmaxl) Xk=Xmaxl;
  if (Yk>Ymaxl) Yk=Ymaxl;
  addset(Xb, Yb); addset(Xk, Yk);
  fclose(fp); cur();
}

blwrite()   /* Write a block (BW) */
{ FILE *fp; int Blength, Bwidth, i, j, X, Y, buflen;
  unsigned char bitbuf[100], *p;
  if (enquire("File: ", str)==0) return;
  delpinblock();
  cur(); fp=fopen(str, "wb");
  Blength=Xk-Xb; Bwidth=Yk-Yb; buflen=(Blength>>3)+1;
  fwrite((char *)&Blength, 1, sizeof(int), fp);
  fwrite((char *)&Bwidth, 1, sizeof(int), fp);
```

```
    for (Y=Yb; Y<=Yk; Y++)
    { for (i=0; i<buflen; i++) bitbuf[i]=0;
      j=0; p=bitbuf;
      for (X=Xb; X<=Xk; X++)
      { *p <<= 1;
        if (pixlit(X, Y)) *p |= 1;
        if (++j == 8) { p++; j=0; }
      }
      *p <<= (8-j);
      fwrite(bitbuf, 1, buflen, fp);
    }
    fclose(fp); cur();
}

clearset()   /* Clear the set of points (SC) */
{ int i;
  struct SET *p;
  if (marksvisible)
  for (i=0; i<n; i++)
  { p = set + i; mark(p->XX, p->YY);
  }
  n=0;
}

static int clipcode(x, y) float x, y;
{ return (x<xmin)<<3 | (x>xmax)<<2 | (y<ymin)<<1 | (y>ymax);
}

static clipdraw(x1, y1, x2, y2) float x1, y1, x2, y2;
{ int c1, c2;
  float dx, dy;
  c1=clipcode(x1, y1); c2=clipcode(x2, y2);
  while (c1|c2)
  { if (c1&c2) return;
    dx=x2-x1; dy=y2-y1;
    if (c1)
    { if (c1 & 8) { y1 += dy*(xmin-x1)/dx; x1=xmin; } else
      if (c1 & 4) { y1 += dy*(xmax-x1)/dx; x1=xmax; } else
      if (c1 & 2) { x1 += dx*(ymin-y1)/dy; y1=ymin; } else
      if (c1 & 1) { x1 += dx*(ymax-y1)/dy; y1=ymax; }
      c1=clipcode(x1, y1);
    } else
    { if (c2 & 8) { y2 += dy*(xmin-x2)/dx; x2=xmin; } else
      if (c2 & 4) { y2 += dy*(xmax-x2)/dx; x2=xmax; } else
      if (c2 & 2) { x2 += dx*(ymin-y2)/dy; y2=ymin; } else
      if (c2 & 1) { x2 += dx*(ymax-y2)/dy; y2=ymax; }
      c2=clipcode(x2, y2);
    }
  }
  move(x1, y1); Xend1=Xcur; Yend1=Ycur; /* to be used in  */
  draw(x2, y2); Xend2=Xcur; Yend2=Ycur; /* lsegment!      */
  Xend1 = fx(x1); Yend1 = fy(y1); /* Used in 'lsegment' */
  Xend2 = fx(x2); Yend2 = fy(y2);
}

coord()   /* Display coordinate values */
{ prnum(160, Xcur); prnum(240, Ycur);
}

cur()     /* Display/erase cursor */
{ int i, j, dm;
  dm=drawmode; drawmode=0; /* change color, using xor */
  for (j=-2; j<=2; j+=4)
  for (i=-4; i<=4; i++) dot(Xcur+i, Ycur+j);
  dot(Xcur-4, Ycur-1); dot(Xcur-3, Ycur-1);
  dot(Xcur+3, Ycur-1); dot(Xcur+4, Ycur-1);
```

```
      dot(Xcur-4, Ycur); dot(Xcur-3, Ycur); dot(Xcur+3, Ycur);
      dot(Xcur+4, Ycur);  dot(Xcur, Ycur);
      dot(Xcur-4, Ycur+1); dot(Xcur-3, Ycur+1);
      dot(Xcur+3, Ycur+1); dot(Xcur+4, Ycur+1);
      drawmode=dm;
}


#define ARSIZE 1004

curvefit(closed) int closed;
{ int ninit, nend, i, j, N=15, first=1, nr[ARSIZE], m;
   float xA, xB, xC, xD, yA, yB, yC, yD, x, y,
      a0, a1, a2, a3, b0, b1, b2, b3, t;
   double fx(), fy();
   struct SET *p;
   ninit = find(XI, YI);      /* If not found in 'set', 'find' returns n */
   nend = find(XE, YE);
   if (nend == n || nend - ninit < 3) { ninit = 0; nend = n - 1; }
   m = nend - ninit;
   if (m < 3) { message("Too few points"); return; }
   if (m + 3 > ARSIZE) { message("Too many points"); return; }
   for (i=0; i <= m; i++) nr[i] = ninit + i;
   if (closed) { nr[++m] = ninit; nr[++m] = ninit+1; nr[++m] = ninit+2; }
   for (i=1; i<m-1; i++)
   { p = set + nr[i-1]; xA = fx(p -> XX); yA = fy(p -> YY);
      p = set + nr[i];    xB = fx(p -> XX); yB = fy(p -> YY);
      p = set + nr[i+1]; xC = fx(p -> XX); yC = fy(p -> YY);
      p = set + nr[i+2]; xD = fx(p -> XX); yD = fy(p -> YY);
      a3=(-xA+3*(xB-xC)+xD)/6.0; b3=(-yA+3*(yB-yC)+yD)/6.0;
      a2=(xA-2*xB+xC)/2.0;       b2=(yA-2*yB+yC)/2.0;
      a1=(xC-xA)/2.0;            b1=(yC-yA)/2.0;
      a0=(xA+4*xB+xC)/6.0;       b0=(yA+4*yB+yC)/6.0;
      for (j=0; j<=N; j++)
      { t=(float)j/(float)N;
         x=((a3*t+a2)*t+a1)*t+a0;
         y=((b3*t+b2)*t+b1)*t+b0;
         if (x > xmin && x < xmax && y > ymin && y < ymax)
         { if (first) { first=0; move(x, y);} else draw(x, y);
         }
      }
   }
}

static dash(x1, y1, x2, y2) float x1, y1, x2, y2;
{ int i, k;
   float xdif=x2-x1, ydif=y2-y1, pitch0=0.3, dx, dy;
   k = 2 * (int)ceil(sqrt(xdif*xdif+ydif*ydif)/pitch0) + 1;
   dx=xdif/k; dy=ydif/k;
   for (i=0; i<k; i+=2)
   { move(x1+i*dx, y1+i*dy); draw(x1+(i+1)*dx, y1+(i+1)*dy);
   }
}

defdirection()   /* Define direction (DD) */
{ enquire("Enter angle or *:", str);
   if (sscanf(str, "%f", &phi) > 0) phi=phi*PI/180.0; else
   { if (!vdefined) { message("Vector?"); return; }
      phi=phi0;
   }
}

static delpinblock() /* Delete all points within block from set */
{ int i, j, X, Y;
   struct SET *p;
   for (i=0; i<n; i++)
```

```
  { p = set+i; X = p->XX; Y=p->YY;
    if (X>=Xb && X<=Xk && Y>=Yb && Y<=Yk)
    if (marksvisible) mark(X, Y);                    /* delete */
    n--;
    for (j=i; j<n; j++) set[j]=set[j+1];
    i--;
  }
}


delpset(Xl, Yl)  /* Remove a point from set (SD) */
{ int i, j;
  i=find(Xl, Yl);
  if (i==n) { message("Not in set"); return; }
  if (marksvisible) mark(Xl, Yl);  /* delete */
  n--;
  for (j=i; j<n; j++) set[j]=set[j+1];
}


dmode(m) int m; /* Change drawing mode (PP, PN, PA) */
/*  1 = Positive,  -1 = Negative,  0 = Alternate  */
{ textXY(0, 55, m == 1 ? "P" : m == -1 ? "N" : "A");
  drawmode = m;
}


drawtoP()    /* Draw line segment (L) */
{ int X, Y;
  if (Xcur==Xprev && Ycur==Yprev)
  { X = XXold; Y = YYold;
  } else
  { X = Xprev; Y = Yprev; addset(Xcur, Ycur);
  }
  if (X<0) message("Previous point?"); else draw_line(X, Y, Xcur, Ycur);
}


endpoint()  /* Define vector endpoint (E) */
{ if (XI == -1) { message("Point I?"); return; }
  if (Xcur==XI && Ycur==YI) { message("Zero vector!"); return; }
  if (vdefined && !keepvector) ievector(); /* delete vector IE    */
  XE=Xcur; YE=Ycur; geometrics(); addset(Xcur, Ycur);
  ievector(); vdefined=1; keepvector=0;
}


static int enquire(txt, str) char *txt, *str;
{ char ch, s[2]; int i=0, len;
  len=strlen(txt);
  message(txt); s[1]='\0';
  while (ch=getch(), ch != '\n' && ch != '\r' && ch != ' ')
  { if (ch==8)
    { if (--i<0) i=0; /* dealing with backspace */
      continue;
    }
    str[i]=s[0]=ch; textXY((len+i+1)<<3, 0, s); i++;
  }
  str[i]='\0';
  return i;
}

static int find(X, Y) int X, Y; /* Find position of (X, Y) in set */
{ struct SET *p;
  p=set+n;
  p->XX = X; p->YY = Y; /* sentinel */
  for (p=set; p->XX != X || p->YY != Y; p++); /* empty statement */
  return p-set;  /* if found, position (<n), otherwise n */
}
```

```
findset() /* Move current point to nearest point in set (F) */
{ int XP, YP;
  struct SET *p;
  float minim2=1.0e10, xl, yl, dx, dy, sq;
  if (n==0) { message("Empty set"); return; }
  xl=fx(Xcur); yl=fy(Ycur);
  for (p=set; p<set+n; p++)
  { dx=fx(p->XX)-xl; dy=fy(p->YY)-yl; sq = dx*dx + dy*dy;
    if (sq<minim2) { minim2=sq; XP = p->XX; YP = p->YY; }
  }
  cur(); Xcur=XP; Ycur=YP; cur(); coord();
  XXold=Xprev; YYold=Yprev;
  Xprev=Xcur; Yprev=Ycur;
}

static double fx(X) int X; { return X/horfact; }
static double fy(Y) int Y; { return (Y__max - Y)/vertfact; }

static geometrics()
/* Computes the global variables
        xxi, yyi, xxe, yye, xxl, yyl, dx, dy, r, phi0, phil */
{ xxi = fx(XI); yyi = fy(YI);
  xxe = fx(XE); yye = fy(YE);
  xxl = fx(Xcur); yyl = fy(Ycur);
  dx = xxe - xxi; dy = yye - yyi;
  r = sqrt(dx * dx + dy * dy);
  phi0 = angle(xxi, yyi, xxe, yye);
  phil = angle(xxi, yyi, xxl, yyl);
}

hardcopy(code) char code;  /* Picture to printer (P0, P1, P2) */
{ int Xlo, Xhi, Ylo, Yhi;  '
  if (code == '2') { Xlo=Ylo=0; Xhi=X__max; Yhi=Y__max; } else
                   { Xlo=Xminl; Xhi=Xmaxl; Ylo=Yminl; Yhi=Ymaxl; }
  if (code == '0') { Xlo++; Xhi--; Ylo++; Yhi--; }
  printgr(Xlo, Xhi, Ylo, Yhi);
}

icursor(XI, YI) int XI, YI;  /* Toggle I-cursor */
{ float xi, yi;
  xi=fx(XI); yi=fy(YI);
  clipdraw(xi-0.1, yi, xi+0.1, yi);
  clipdraw(xi, yi-0.1, xi, yi+0.1);
}

static ievector()
{ draw_line(XI, YI, XE, YE); arrow();
}

invalid()  /* Display error message */
{ message("Invalid character");
}

inviset()   /* Make points in set invisible/visible (SI) */
{ struct SET *p;
  for (p=set; p<set+n; p++) { mark(p->XX, p->YY); }
  marksvisible ^= 1;
}

ipoint() /* Initial point of vector (I) */
{ if (XI != -1) icursor(XI, YI);              /* delete cursor at I */
  if (vdefined && !keepvector) ievector(); /* delete vector IE   */
  vdefined=0;
  XI=Xcur; YI=Ycur; icursor(XI, YI);
  addset(Xcur, Ycur);
}
```

```
static int load()
{ int i=-1, j;
  short bufar[13];
  unsigned char buf, ncopies;
  FILE *fp;
  fp=fopen(fil, "rb");
  if (fp == NULL) return 0;
  if (fread((char *)bufar, 2, 13, fp) < 13) { fclose(fp); return 0; }
  XI=bufar[0]; YI=bufar[1]; XE=bufar[2]; YE=bufar[3];
  Xcur=bufar[4]; Ycur=bufar[5]; Xb=bufar[6]; Yb=bufar[7];
  Xk=bufar[8]; Yk=bufar[9]; marksvisible=bufar[10]; n=bufar[11];
  vdefined=bufar[12];
  if (fread((char *)set, sizeof (struct SET), n, fp) < n)
  { fclose(fp); return 0;
  }
  do
  { if (fread(&buf, 1, 1, fp) == 0) { fclose(fp); return 0; }
    poke(0xB800, ++i, &buf, 1);
    if (buf == 0 || buf == 0xFF)
    { fread(&ncopies, 1, 1, fp);
      if (buf)
      { for (j=0; j<ncopies; j++) poke(0xB800, ++i, &buf, 1);
      } else i+=ncopies;
    }
  } while (i < displaymax);
  fclose(fp); return 1;
}


lseg() /* Sketch horizontal or vertical line segment (PD etc.):
  if pendown, draw line segment from (Xold, Yold) to (Xcur, Ycur) */
{ static int prevdown,
      /* Was previously a line segment drawn to old point? */
    prevdirection, direction;
  if (pendown)
  { draw_line(Xold, Yold, Xcur, Ycur);
    direction = Xcur < Xold ? -1 :
                Xcur > Xold ?  1 :
                Ycur < Yold ? -2 :
                Ycur > Yold ?  2 : 0;
    /* If prevdirection + direction == 0, and drawmode == 0, a line
       segment just drawn is erased; beware of an extra call of dot
       in the point of reversal, performed in  draw_line. */
    if (prevdown && drawmode==0 && prevdirection + direction == 0)
      dot(Xold, Yold); /* fourth call of dot in (Xold, Yold) */
  }
  prevdown = pendown; prevdirection = direction;
}


lsegment(code) int code; /* (VS (0), VD(1), VL(2) */
/* code 0: drawn segment,  1: dashed segment,  2: long line */
{ int XX1, YY1, XX2, YY2;
  if (vdefined)
  { arrow();           /* delete arrow        */
    icursor(XI, YI); /* delete cursor at I */
    if (code)
    { draw_line(XI, YI, XE, YE); /* delete line segment */
      if (code==1) dash(xxi, yyi, xxe, yye); else
      { float c, s;
        c=10.0*cos(phi0); s=10.0*sin(phi0);
        clipdraw(xxi-c, yyi-s, xxi+c, yyi+s);
        /* 'clipdraw' computes Xend1, Yend1, Xend2, Yend2 */
        XX1=Xend1; YY1=Yend1;
        XX2=Xend2; YY2=Yend2; /* Local copies (XX2, YY2) are    */
```

```
            addset(XX1, YY1);      /* needed for reasons of security */
            addset(XX2, YY2);
       }
    }
    vdefined=0; XI=-1;
  } else message("No vector");
}

static mark(X, Y) int X, Y;
{ float x, y, dx=0.07, dy=0.07;
  x=fx(X); y=fy(Y);
  clipdraw(x-dx, y-dy, x+dx, y+dy);
  clipdraw(x-dx, y+dy, x+dx, y-dy);
}

message(str) char *str;  /* Erase old message and display new one */
{ textXY(8, 0, "                                            ");
  textXY(8, 0, str);
}

newpoint() /* Find a new point in a given direction (DN) */
{ float d0, d, cphi, sphi, xold=-1000.0, yold, xnew=-1000, ynew;
  int XX, YY;
  if (phi>100.0) { message("Angle undefined"); return; }
  xold=fx(Xcur); yold=fy(Ycur); cphi=cos(phi); sphi=sin(phi);
  if (find(Xcur, Ycur)==n) addset(Xcur, Ycur);
                                    /* add to set if not yet in it */
  enquire("Length, or *:", str);
  if (sscanf(str,"%f", &d0) > 0) d=d0*un; else
  { if (!vdefined) { message("Vector?"); return; }
    d = -(xold*yyi+yold*xxe+xxi*yye-xxe*yyi-xxi*yold-xold*yye)/
         (cphi*yyi+sphi*xxe-xxi*sphi-yye*cphi);
    /* Now (xold+d*cos(phi), yold+d*sin(phi)) is the point of intersection
       we are interested in */
  }
  xnew=xold+d*cphi; ynew=yold+d*sphi;
  XX=IX(xnew); YY=IY(ynew);
  if (XX<Xmin1 || XX>Xmax1 || YY<Ymin1 || YY>Ymax1)
    message("Outside screen"); else
  { cur(); Xcur=XX; Ycur=YY; cur(); coord();
    addset(Xcur, Ycur);
  }
}


penposition(p) int p; /* Display pen position:  1 = down,  0 = up */
{ int dm;
  dm=drawmode; drawmode=1;
  textXY(0, p ? 27 : 40, "  ");   /* clear old pen portion */
  textXY(0, p ? 32 : 27, "H");
  textXY(0, p ? 40 : 35, "V");    /* a picture of a pen */
  draw_line(0, 48, 6, 48);    /* the paper on which the pen writes */
  pendown=p; drawmode=dm;
}

prnum(X, num) int X, num;  /* Display a number in bottom margin */
{ char str[4];
  sprintf(str, "%3d", num); textXY(X, Ybottext, str);
}

save()  /* Write entire picture to file */
{ int i=-1;
  short bufar[13];
  unsigned char ncopies, buf, newbuf;
  FILE *fp;
  fp=fopen(fil, "wb");
```

```
     if (fp==NULL) { invalid(); return; }
     bufar[0]=XI; bufar[1]=YI; bufar[2]=XE; bufar[3]=YE;
     bufar[4]=Xcur; bufar[5]=Ycur; bufar[6]=Xb; bufar[7]=Yb;
     bufar[8]=Xk; bufar[9]=Yk; bufar[10]=marksvisible; bufar[11]=n;
     bufar[12]=vdefined;
     fwrite((char *)bufar, 2, 13, fp);
     fwrite((char *)set, sizeof(struct SET), n, fp);
     do
     { peek(0xB800, ++i, &buf, 1);
       fwrite(&buf, 1, 1, fp);
       if (buf == 0 || buf == 0xFF)
       { ncopies=0; /* ncopies = number of extra copies */
         if (i < displaymax)
         { while (peek(0xB800, ++i, &newbuf, 1), newbuf==buf)
           { ncopies++;
             if (i == displaymax || ncopies == 0xFF) break;
           }
           if (newbuf != buf) i--;
         }
         fwrite(&ncopies, 1, 1, fp); /* ncopies may be 0 */
       }
     } while (i < displaymax);
     fclose(fp);
}

static togrmode()   /* Switch to graphics mode, called in 'wstate' */
{ static int load_desired=1;
  initgr();
  displaymax = (colorgr ? 16383 : 32767);
  Xmin1 = 12; Xmax1 = X__max - 4; Ymin1 = 22; Ymax1 = Y__max - 14;
  xmin=fx(Xmin1); xmax=fx(Xmax1);
  ymin=fy(Ymax1); ymax=fy(Ymin1);
  drawmode=1;
  if (load_desired)
  { if (!load())
    { /* Completely new drawing: */
      draw_line(Xmin1, Ymin1, Xmax1, Ymin1);
      draw_line(Xmax1, Ymin1, Xmax1, Ymax1);
      draw_line(Xmax1, Ymax1, Xmin1, Ymax1);
      draw_line(Xmin1, Ymax1, Xmin1, Ymin1);
      Xcur=Ycur=30; cur();
    }
  }
  Ybottext = Ymax1 +3; textXY(8, Ybottext, "Stepsize:");
  textXY(128, Ybottext, "X =");
  textXY(208, Ybottext, "Y =");
  coord(); prnum(80, stsize);
  load_desired = colorgr;
}

toseq(code) int code;
{ int i;
  if (n == 0) { message("Empty set"); return; }
  if (abs(code) == 1 && (i = find(Xcur, Ycur)) == n)
  { message("Use F first"); return;
  }
  cur();                                /* Delete old cursor */
  switch (code)
  { case -2: i = 0; break;
    case  2: i = n-1; break;
    case -1: if (i > 0) i--; break;
    case  1: if (i < n - 1) i++; break;
  }
  Xcur = set[i].XX; Ycur = set[i].YY;
  XXold=Xprev; YYold=Yprev;
  Xprev=Xcur; Yprev=Ycur;
  cur(); return;
}
```

```
static totextmode()    /* Called in wstate */
{ to_text(); menu('M');
}

unit()  /* Define unit of length (DU) */
{ int n;
  float dx, dy;
  if (!vdefined) { message("No initial point"); return; }
  if (XE==XI && YE==YI) { message("Zero vector"); return; }
  enquire("How many units?", str);
  sscanf(str, "%d", &n); if (n<=0) n=1;
  dx=fx(XE)-fx(XI); dy=fy(YE)-fy(YI);
  un=sqrt(dx*dx+dy*dy)/n;
}

wstate(ch) char ch;  /* New workstate (WA, WL, WT),
                          'ch' is new state, 'workstate' is old state */
{ if (ch=='T')
  { if (workstate=='T') printf("Already in textmode\n"); else
    { if (colorgr) save();
      /* So that load() can be used when reverting to graphics mode later
         (the screen then having been blanked by the
          BIOS routine for the color graphics card). */
      totextmode();
    }
  } else
  { if (workstate=='T') togrmode(); /* Switch to graphics mode */
    textXY(8, 11,
    ch =='L' ? "Line-drawing state.  " :
               "Graphics alpha state.");
    textXY(344, 0,  (ch=='A'?"Use Ctrl WT for text mode":
    "Use WT for text mode      "));
    penposition(0); /* up     */
    dmode(0);       /* toggle */
  }
  workstate=ch;
}
```

6.5.3 Program text of DIGH.C (help messages)

```
/* DIGH.C: Functions for help, used in DIG.C.              */

static p(s) char *s; { printf(s); }

menu(ch) char ch;
{ int again=1;
  while(again)
  { switch (ch)
    {
      case 'M': p("\n\n\n\n\n\n\n\n\n\n\n");

p("Drawing with Interactive Graphics, by L. Ammeraal.\n");
p("Published by John Wiley & Sons, Chichester/New york\n\n\n");
p("Main Menu:\n\n");
p("Enter one of the following commands:\n\n");
p("WL      : Switch to line-drawing workstate.\n");
p("WA      : Switch to graphics alpha workstate.\n");
p("Q       : Quit; graphics results will be saved.\n");
p("Ctrl C : Quit immediately.\n");
p("H       : Help.\n"); break;

      case 'H': p("\n\n\n\n\n\n\n\n\n\n\n\nHelp Menu:\n\n");

p("Press:\n\n");
p("1   for program start and state switching\n");
```

```
p("2    for cursor commands, pen position and drawing modes\n");
p("3    for the alpha workstate\n");
p("4    for commands to manipulate a set of marked points\n");
p("5    for block commands\n");
p("6    for vectors, circles and arcs\n");
p("7    for directions, units of length, new points\n");
p("8    for matrix printer usage and for area filling\n");
p("9    for B-spline curve fitting\n");
p("M    to return to the main menu\n\n");
p("After that, you may enter another digit to");
                    p(" display a group of commands,\n");
p("or press M or H to display the main or help menu once again.");
                break;

        case '1': p("\n\n\n\n\n\n");

p("1. Program start and state switching\n");
p("=====================================\n\n");
p("DIG     : Start the program; dimensions are");
                    p(" based on the screen.\n");
p("DIG -P  : Start the program;");
    p(" dimensions are based on the matrix printer.\n\n\n");
p("Angles will have their proper sizes and");
                    p(" circles will appear as circles\n");
p("on the printer if the option  -P is used.");
p(" If proper dimensions on the\n");
p("screen are more important than those on the printer,");
                    p(" the option -P should\n");
p("not be used.\n\n");
p("WL      : Switch to line-drawing state.\n");
p("WA      : Switch to graphics alpha state.\n");
p("WT      : Switch to text state, to quit, or to ask for help.\n\n");
p("Note:  In graphics alpha state the Control key must\n");
p("       be kept down when the letter W is entered for\n");
p("       state switching.\n"); break;

        case '2': p("\n\n\n\n\n\n\n");

p("2. Cursor commands, pen position and drawing modes\n");
p("==================================================\n\n");
p("\nThe cursor is moved by pressing the arrow keys.\n");
p("The step size is increased or decreased");
                    p(" by pressing > or <.\n\n");
p("PU :  Pen Up\n");
p("PD :  Pen Down\n");
p("PP :  Pen in Positive drawing mode:");
                    p(" use pen, when down, to draw.\n");
p("PN :  Pen in Negative drawing mode:");
                    p(" use pen, when down, to rub out.\n");
p("PA :  Pen in Alternate drawing mode:");
                    p(" use pen, when down, to toggle.\n\n");
p("The following commands may have confusing effects,");
                    p(" so be cautious when\n");
p("using them:\n\n");
p("* :  Toggle cursor\n");
p(". :  Toggle dot\n");
p("+ :  Toggle I-cursor\n"); break;

        case '3': p("\n\n\n\n\n\n\n\n\n\n\n");

p("3. The alpha workstate\n");
p("======================\n\n");
p("Text appears in the drawing as it is entered.");
                    p(" The backspace key\n");
p("may be used for corrections. Keep the Ctrl key");
                    p(" down when pressing\n");
```

```
p("the first letter W of the state switching commands");
                    p(" WT, WL.\n"); break;

        case '4': p("\n\n\n\n\n");

p("4. Commands to manipulate a set of marked points\n");
p("===================================================\n\n");
p("All points in the set are marked X.\n\n");
p("SA :  Add point to set.\n");
p("SD :  Delete point from set.\n");
p("SC :  Clear the set.\n");
p("SI :  Toggle points in set (invisible/visible).\n");
p("F  :  Find the nearest point in the set,");
                    p(" and move cursor to it.\n");
p("L  :  Use the point most recently added to the set");
                    p(" as the 'old' point.\n");
p("       Then a line segment is drawn from the old point");
                    p(" to the current\n");
p("       cursor position. Besides SA, the commands L,");
                    p(" I also add points\n");
p("       to the set.\n");
p("(See also 9.)\n"); break;

        case '5': p("\n\n\n\n\n\n");

p("5. Block commands\n");
p("=================\n\n");
p("BB : Begin of block, top-left corner.\n");
p("BK : End of block, bottom-right corner.\n");
p("BE : Erase (or draw again) block boundary.\n");
p("BD : Delete the entire block.\n");
p("BC : Block Copy.\n");
p("BM : Block Move.\n");
p("BW : Block Write.\n");
p("BR : Block Read.\n"); break;

        case '6': p("\n\n\n\n\n");

p("6. Vectors, circles and arcs\n");
p("============================\n\n");
p("I :   Define initial point I of vector.\n");
p("E :   Define vector endpoint E of vector.\n\n");
p("VA :  Toggle arrow of vector (invisible/visible).\n");
p("VS :  Replace vector with line segment.\n");
p("VD :  Replace vector with dashed line segment.\n");
p("VL :  Replace vector with long line.\n");
p("VK :  Keep vector: the arrow is to be permanent.\n\n");
p("With CF, C+, C-, point point I is the center and IE the radius.\n");
p("CF : Draw a full circle.\n");
p("C+ : Draw arc with a given angle, counter-clockwise.\n");
p("C- : Similarly, clockwise.\n");
p("       With C+ and C-, if the cursor is not in E,");
                    p(" its position will be\n");
p("       used to determine the angle of the arc.\n"); break;

        case '7': p("\n\n\n\n\n");

p("7. Directions, units of length, new points\n");
p("==========================================\n\n");
p("The following three commands ask for a number");
                    p(" of an asterisk. Don't\n");
p("forget to press the Enter key after");
                    p(" typing that number or asterisk.\n\n");
p("DU :  When this command is used, a vector IE must");
                    p(" have been defined.\n");
p("       The question 'How many units?' is displayed.");
                    p(" If you now enter\n");
```

```
p("      some integer value n, the unit of length is");
              p(" defined such that\n");
p("      the length of IE is n, expressed in this unit.");
              p(" The unit may be\n");
p("      used by subsequent DN commands.\n\n");
p("DD :  An angle measured from the positive X-axis");
              p(" is requested to define\n");
p("      a direction. This direction will be used");
              p(" by subsequent DN commands.\n");
p("      An asterisk means: use the direction of");
              p(" vector IE for this purpose.\n\n");
p("DN :  Find a new point in the current direction, at a given\n");
p("      distance from the current cursor position.\n");
p("      An asterisk means: place the point on the line IE.\n");
              break;

       case '8': p("\n\n\n\n\n\n");

p("8. Output on a matrix printer; area filling\n");
p("=============================================\n\n");
p("P0 :  Print everything inside the window");
              p(" boundaries (not the boundaries\n");
p("      themselves).\n");
p("P1 :  Print everything inside the boundaries, including the\n");
p("      boundaries  themselves.\n");
p("P2 :  Print the complete screen.\n\n");
p("PF :  Fill the closed region in which the cursor is lying.");
              p(" Beware of\n");
p("      'bleeding', which will happen if the region is");
              p(" not completely\n");
p("      closed. Before giving the command PF,");
              p(" temporarily erase any marks,\n");
p("      using SI.\n"); break;

       case '9':

p("\n\n9. B-spline curve fitting\n");
p("=========================\n");
p("The set of marked points is now regarded as a sequence.\n\n");
p("S< : Move the cursor to the initial point of the sequence.\n");
p("S> : Move the cursor to the final point of the sequence.\n");
p("S[ : Move the cursor to the predecessor of the");
              p(" current marked point.\n");
p("S] : Move the cursor to the successor of the current");
              p(" marked point.\n\n");
p("SF : Draw (or erase) a curve that approximately");
              p(" passes through the\n");
p("      marked points, with the exception of the initial");
              p(" and the final");
p("      point.\n");
p("SR : As SF, but now going round, drawing a closed curve.\n\n");
p("If I and E coincide with appropriate points of");
              p(" the sequence, the\n");
p("subsequence beginning in I and ending in E is used");
              p(" instead of the\n");
p("entire sequence of marked points.");
              p(" (IE will be shown as an arrow.)\n\n");
p("The sequence can be updated using SD and SA (see 4.).");
              p(" After moving\n");
p("the cursor to a marked point (using F, ], or [),");
              p(" you can insert a new\n");
p("point immediately after that marked point by moving");
              p(" the cursor to the\n");
p("new point and using SA.\n"); break;
```

```
      case ' ': case '\n': break;
      default: again=0; ungetch(ch);
   }
   if (again)
   { ch = getche(); ch = toupper(ch);
   }
  }
}
```

APPENDIX A

GRPACK summary

Programmers using Lattice C, Version 3, can link their compiled programs together with GRPACK.OBJ, and use the graphics facilities summarized below. Programs compiled and linked in this way run under PC DOS or MS DOS on any IBM (compatible) PC with either the color graphics or the (Hercules compatible) monochrome graphics adapter.

We distinguish between real screen coordinates (inches), denoted by small letters x, y, and integer pixel coordinates, denoted by capital letters X, Y. The origin ($x = 0.0$, $y = 0.0$) of the real coordinate system lies in the bottom-left corner of the screen:

$$0.0 \leqq x \leqq x\_max$$
$$0.0 \leqq y \leqq y\_max$$

The values of x_max and y_max are 10.0 and 7.0, respectively, unless the function *setprdim( )* is called, see below. The origin ($X = 0$, $Y = 0$) of the pixel coordinate system lies in the top-left corner of the screen:

$$0 \leqq X \leqq X\_\_max$$
$$0 \leqq Y \leqq Y\_\_max$$

The values of $X\_\_max$ and $Y\_\_max$ are as follows:

	$X\_\_max$	$Y\_\_max$
Color graphics adapter:	639	199
Monochrome graphics adapter:	719	347

The variables x_max, y_max, $X\_\_max$, $Y\_\_max$ are defined in GRPACK. We can use their values by declaring:

```
extern float x_max, y_max;
extern int X__max, Y__max;
```

The following list shows the graphics functions that are available, with a short description. It also shows the meaning of the arguments, if any. You are referred to my book for more information.

initgr( )	Initialize graphics; the video displays switches to graphics mode. With the exception of *setprdim( )*, all other graphics functions may be used only after calling *initgr( )*.
endgr( )	Wait until a key is pressed; then the video display returns to text mode. Don't forget to call this function (or *to_text*) before program termination.
to_text( )	Return to textmode immediately.

move(*x, y*)   Move a fictitious pen to (*x, y*) (real coordinates).
imove(*X, Y*)   Move pen to (*X, Y*) (pixel coordinates).
draw(*x, y*)   Draw line segment from old pen position to new pen position (*x, y*).
idraw(*X, Y*)   Draw line segment from old pen position to new pen position (*X, Y*).
draw_line(*X*1, *Y*1, *X*2, *Y*2)
                Draw line segment from (*X*1, *Y*1) to (*X*2, *Y*2). (No change in current pen position)
circle(*xC, yC, r*)   Draw a circle with center (*xC, yC*) and radius *r*.
dot(*X, Y*)   Place a dot in point (*X, Y*).

We can erase lines, circles and dots by declaring

```
extern int drawmode;
```

and assigning the value −1 to this variable *drawmode*. The functions *draw, idraw, draw_line, circle, dot* will then turn pixels dark. By default, *drawmode* is equal to 1, which causes these functions to light pixels. As a third option, we can 'toggle' pixels by assigning the value 0 to *drawmode*. In that case these functions will light the pixels involved if they are dark, and darken them if they are lit. This discussion does not apply to the remaining functions:

clearpage( )   Clear the screen.
fill(*x, y*)   Fill the closed region in which (*x, y*) lies with lit pixels. Beware of 'bleeding' in case the region is not completely closed!
pixfill(*X, Y*)   Fill the closed region in which (*X, Y*) lies with lit pixels. Be cautious!
text(*str*)   While in graphics mode, display string *str*, starting in the current pen position (probably obtained by calling *imove* or *move*). Section 5.6 shows how we can use this function to display newly designed characters.
textXY(*X, Y, str*)   The same as *text*(*str*), except for the starting point, which is now given explicitly.
printgr(*Xlo, Xhi, Ylo, Yhi*)
                Print the (graphics) contents of rectangle *Xlo* ≤ *X* ≤ *Xhi*, *Ylo* ≤ *Y* ≤ *Yhi*. A matrix printer must be connected to the parallel printer port and switched on. See also *setprdim*( ).
                (For the monochrome graphics adapter, *printgr*( ) may be used not only in graphics mode but also in text mode!)
setprdim( )   'Set print dimensions'. If we call this function prior to *initgr*( ), the horizontal and vertical dimensions will be printed correctly later. This function should not be used if optimal results on the screen are required.

The following two functions return an integer value:

pixlit(X, Y)	Returns 1 if pixel (X, Y) is lit and 0 if it is dark.
iscolor( )	Returns a code for the graphics adapter that is being used:

   1: color graphics,
   0: monochrome graphics,
 -1: no graphics adapter.

APPENDIX B

A mouse as a graphics input device

If you use an IBM (compatible) PC with a mouse, you may be interested in how to obtain input data from this device in your graphics programs. The following program shows this in a simple way. It assumes that the Microsoft mouse driver has been installed. This is a program called *msmouse*, which you probably have bought together with the mouse. The function *mouse* in the program below shows that we use software interrupt 51 (33H) for this purpose.

```
/* MOUSEDEM.C: Demonstration of a mouse.                           */
/*             After compilation, this program should be linked */
/*             together with GRPACK.OBJ.                           */

#include "dos.h"
extern int drawmode, X__max, Y__max;   /* Defined in GRPACK.C */

main()
{ int buttons, Xm, Ym, X0, Y0, X, Y, Xdev, Ydev, Xmin, Xmax, Ymin, Ymax;
  printf("This program assumes that the Microsoft mouse driver has\n");
  printf("been loaded (program  'msmouse' should have been executed).\n");
  printf("If not, use Ctrl Break.\n\n");
  printf("The program demonstrates how x- and y-coordinates can\n");
  printf("be derived from the position of the mouse. You can draw\n");
  printf("curves with this program.\n\n");
  printf("Press any key on the keyboard to start the demonstration.\n");
  printf("The demonstration ends in the same way.\n");
  /* For each button on the mouse there is a bit in the variable */
  /* 'button', which is set as long as the button is pressed.     */
  /* The buttons are not used in this program.                    */
  getch();
  initgr();
  Xmin = 4; Xmax = X__max - 4;
  Ymin = 2; Ymax = Y__max - 2;
  drawmode=0;
  mouse(0, &buttons, &Xm, &Ym);   /* Initialize mouse      */
  mouse(3, &buttons, &Xm, &Ym);   /* Read initial position */
  X = (X__max + 1)/2; Y = (Y__max + 1)/2;
  Xdev = X - Xm; Ydev = Y - Ym;
  cursor(X, Y);
  do
  { mouse(3, &buttons, &Xm, &Ym);
    X0 = X; Y0 = Y;
    X = Xm + Xdev; Y = Ym + Ydev;
    if (X < Xmin) X = Xmin;
    if (X > Xmax) X = Xmax;
    if (Y < Ymin) Y = Ymin;
    if (Y > Ymax) Y = Ymax;
    cursor(X0, Y0);                     /* Erase old cursor     */
    cursor(X, Y);                       /* Draw new cursor      */
    draw_line(X0, Y0, X, Y);            /* Draw line segment    */
  } while (!kbhit());
  to_text();
}
```

```
mouse(code, pbuttons, px, py) int code, *pbuttons, *px, *py;
{ union REGS regs;
  regs.x.ax=code; regs.x.bx=*pbuttons; regs.x.cx=*px; regs.x.dx=*py;
  int86(51, &regs, &regs);
  *pbuttons=regs.x.bx;
  *px=regs.x.cx;
  *py=regs.x.dx;
}

cursor(X, Y) int X, Y;
{ imove(X-4, Y-2); idraw(X+4, Y-2); idraw(X+4, Y+2); idraw(X-4, Y+2);
  idraw(X-4, Y-2);
}
```

Bibliography

Ammeraal, L. (1986) *Programming Principles in Computer Graphics,* Chichester: John Wiley & Sons.

Ammeraal, L. (1986) *C for Programmers,* Chichester: John Wiley & Sons.

Foley, J. D., and A. van Dam (1982) *Fundamentals of Interactive Computer Graphics,* Reading, Mass.: Addison-Wesley.

IBM Corporation (1983) *Technical Reference,* Boca Raton, Fl.: IBM Corporation.

Newman, M. N., and R. F. Sproull (1979) *Principles of Interactive Computer Graphics,* New York: McGraw-Hill.

Norton, P. (1983) *Inside the IBM PC,* Bowie, MD.: Brady.

Rogers, D. F. (1985) *Procedural Elements for Computer Graphics,* New York: McGraw-Hill.

Sargent, M., and R. L. Shoemaker (1984) *The IBM Personal Computer from the Inside Out,* Reading, Mass.: Addison-Wesley.

Index